SPIRITUAL POWER

POWER

for your

FAMILY

BEVERLY LaHaye

Charisma
HOUSE
A STRANG COMPANY

Most STRANG COMMUNICATIONS/CHARISMA HOUSE/SILOAM products are available at special quantity discounts for bulk purchase for sales promotions, premiums, fund-raising, and educational needs. For details, write Strang Communications/Charisma House/Siloam, 600 Rinehart Road, Lake Mary, Florida 32746, or telephone (407) 333-0600.

SPIRITUAL POWER FOR YOUR FAMILY by Beverly LaHaye
Published by Charisma House
A Strang Company
600 Rinehart Road
Lake Mary, Florida 32746
www.charismahouse.com

Unless otherwise noted, all Scripture quotations are from the New King James Version of the Bible. Copyright © 1979, 1980, 1982 by Thomas Nelson, Inc., publishers. Used by permission.

Scripture quotations marked KJV are from the King James Version of the Bible.

Scripture quotations marked NIV are from the Holy Bible, New International Version. Copyright © 1973, 1978, 1984, International Bible Society. Used by permission.

Scripture quotations marked RSV are from the Revised Standard Version of the Bible. Copyright © 1946, 1952, 1971 by the Division of Christian Education of the National Council of the Churches of Christ in the USA. Used by permission.

Cover design by Judith McKittrick

Library of Congress Cataloging-in-Publication Data

LaHaye, Beverly.
  Spiritual power for your family / Beverly LaHaye.
     p. cm.
  ISBN 1-59185-656-6
  1. Family-Religious life. 2. Holy Spirit. I. Title.
  BV4526.3.L34 2005
248.4-dc22
                                2004022533

Portions of this book were adapted from SPIRIT-CONTROLLED FAMILY LIVING by Tim and Beverly LaHaye, ISBN 0800709519, copyright © 1978, Fleming H. Revell, Co.

05 06 07 08 09 — 987654321
Printed in the United States of America

This book is lovingly and prayerfully dedicated to the couples who long for a happy and blessed relationship with each other and with their children. It is possible with the help of the Holy Spirit.

Contents

Foreword

WHEN BEVERLY AND I were married in 1947, we were dedicated Christians. Both of us expected to enjoy a fulfilling marriage and a rich family life. We didn't have any reason to think otherwise.

But as the years went along, we began to become disillusioned. We completed our education and plunged into pastoring our first church. Over the next several years, our four children—Linda, Larry, Lee, and Lori—were born. To outward appearances, our life was very good.

The truth was that we were struggling. By the time we had been married ten or twelve years, we had become two strong-willed personalities of the opposite sex who lived in the same house, shared the same children, and held the same basic spiritual views and values, but who disagreed on almost everything else.

Something was missing, and we didn't know what it was. Like many others, we found that we could always exemplify the Christian life when we were away from home, because difficulties came in shorter and less-pressured doses. But at home (where our real selves came out), the pressure was too intense. Clearly, knowing what marriage and family life was supposed to look like wasn't the same as understanding how to live it.

God knew we needed His help more than we knew it, so He intervened. In 1963 we encountered the power of the Holy Spirit at a Forest Home Sunday school conference. Our lives have never been the same since then. In fact, it is doubtful that our many years of marriage could have lasted without the life-changing power of the Holy Spirit.

Gradually, as we yielded control to God, our selfishness, my anger, Bev's fears, and our joint bullheadedness have been replaced by the love, joy, and peace of the Holy Spirit. Now, because of the way He worked with us as we raised our children, we are convinced that the key to happy marriage and family living is the filling of the Holy Spirit.

We are grateful that we discovered the power of the Holy Spirit while our children were still young. However, He can redeem family life at any stage, which is why there is a continual need for the message of this book. Our own "nest" has been empty of our four children for many years, but our home is still full of the love, joy, and peace that come from obeying the Holy Spirit.

Have you allowed the Holy Spirit to take control of your life? Has He filled you—but not your spouse? Have you invited Him to fill your marriage and, by extension, your family life? It's a simple transaction with profound and long-lasting consequences.

The Holy Spirit always enriches and beautifies the life He fills. What better gift can He bestow upon a Christian than to make his home the most wonderful place on earth? That is exactly what He wants to do for all of us. In this book, Beverly holds marriage and family life up to the light to show you how every facet can reflect the beauty of the kingdom of God. I am so glad that Beverly has written *Spiritual Power for Your Family*, because these principles will enable you to enjoy more of God's blessings in your home.

—TIM LaHaye

The Holy Spirit and You

S HOW ME A person who enjoys a happy family life, and I will show you a basically happy person. Show me a child who has been raised in a happy family, and you will find that he or she is secure, productive, more teachable, and always growing. Family fulfillment leads to life fulfillment. More important than peer groups, schools, or the church, the family (for better or for worse) is central to the formation of a child's character and moral values.

Millions of couples can testify that happy marriage and happy family life, which always go hand in hand, cannot be sustained apart from a relationship with God. When I talk about God, I do not mean a stern, rule-oriented deity, but rather a loving Father who has made Himself known through His Son, Jesus. Through Jesus, who is very much alive today, we can receive the same Holy Spirit who inspired everything we read in the Bible. Biblical principles alone, true as they

1

are, are not living principles until the power of the Holy Spirit brings them to life. Without the Holy Spirit, you may be able to understand them, but you cannot practically apply them. With the Holy Spirit, however, you will have a permanent Counselor inside you who will help you every step of the way. The Holy Spirit will guide you through the tough times and reward you with the blessed times.

We need the Father, the Son—and the Holy Spirit. We need the Word of God—and the Holy Spirit. We need to know the truth—and we need to know the Holy Spirit. Abundant life for you, your spouse, and your children comes only from the life of the Holy Spirit within your hearts.

For instance, did you know that self-control, which is mentioned in Galatians 5:22 as part of the fruit of the Spirit, was meant to be *Spirit-controlled* self-control? For the first years of our marriage, Tim and I didn't know that. The truth is that the Christian life is a *supernatural* life, and living it requires supernatural power. We can't live our lives by supernatural standards if we are using only our insufficient and inconsistent natural strength. And our home life is the proving ground.

ANY FAMILY, ANYWHERE

Perhaps you were not raised in a Spirit-filled family. Maybe you feel trapped by your past or consider your current marriage and family life to be a hopelessly tangled situation. Possibly you are a single parent, raising your children alone. Can you experience the power of the Spirit, too? Even though this book is addressed to both parents, the Holy Spirit is not limited by your circumstances. He works through us as individuals.

However, you must do one thing first of all: you must ask Jesus to be Lord of your life. If you have not yet had the life-changing experience that many Christians call being "born again," you can turn to God right now. Tell Him you want to turn over the reins of your life to the Lord Jesus. Ask Him to forgive your sin and save your soul. Ask Him to fill you with His Holy Spirit. After you ask Him to do this, He can start to give you every bit of wisdom and divine assistance you will need to succeed in your life.

You can be sure that He will come into your life, because He has promised to give His Holy Spirit to those who ask Him. Here's His promise, in Jesus' own words:

> Which of you fathers, if your son asks for a fish, will give him a snake instead? Or if he asks for an egg, will give him a scorpion? If you then, though you are evil, know how to give good gifts to your children, how much more will your Father in heaven give the Holy Spirit to those who ask him!
> —LUKE 11:11, NIV

To get started on your adventure of discovery (or to restart it if you have stalled out), you can pray something like this:

> *Dear God,*
>
> *I [re]dedicate my life to Jesus. I want Him to become not only my personal Savior, the One through whom my sins are forgiven, but also the source of the Spirit who will enable me to live His new life.*
>
> *Holy Spirit, I invite You to come and fill me up. I want You to make a difference in everything—in my personal life, in my marriage, in my spiritual walk with You, in my professional life, and in my family life.*
>
> *I commit myself to You, Father, and to the guidance of Your Holy Spirit. I submit to You all that I am, my gifts and talents, and all that You have given me to accomplish. Fill all of it with Your Spirit.*
>
> *Thank You for receiving my prayer and for answering it. Thank You for creating me to love You. Thank You for Your ongoing work in my life.*
>
> *All because of Jesus, amen.*

Come with me through the following chapters as we explore the marvelous results of the fullness of the Holy Spirit in your marriage and family life.

Part One

The Spirit-Empowered Family

CHAPTER 1

The Holy Spirit and Your Family

ALL OF US want to be happy—and loved passionately. Songwriters seem to sing about nothing else. Novelists concentrate their attention on it. From our youth, we pursue it. Advertisers know that they can sell everything from ice cream to real estate if they entice the public with a little romance.

When a man and a woman decide to get married, they expect to be entering into a deeper level of happiness than they possess in their unmarried state. They would never ask a pastor to marry them "because we want to be miserable for the rest of our lives."

When Tim and I married, we thought this would be the beginning of "utopia" and would bring the joy and contentment that young people dream about. After all, we loved each other—what more could we ask? It lasted for a season, but shortly the differences of two people began to cause tension and stress, and discord came into the harmonious dream.

We both grew up without clear examples to follow. My father died when I was two years old, and later my mother remarried. Although my stepfather meant well, he did not know how to bring the joy and peaceful harmony into the home that I desperately wanted. Tim lost his father in death when he was only ten years old, so he too did not have the example of a loving father.

Most adults are like we were, unaware of the pitfalls, approaching marriage as a significant key to happiness, expecting matrimony to usher in that fairy-tale refrain, "And they lived happily ever after." Although a quick look at the divorce statistics will indicate that, realistically, wedlock is a calculated risk, we are willing to try it anyway.

I'm here to say that it *can* be a happily-ever-after experience. Even though it sounds too good to be true, with God's power and your cooperation, your marriage can become a miniature heaven on earth.

THE MARRIAGE CONNECTION

Why am I starting a book about family life by writing about marriage? Simply because a husband and wife cannot have a happy family if they don't have a happy marriage. You can't have one without the other; it's like trying to build a house without a foundation. A couple with unresolved conflicts may beget several children, but they cannot be good parents unless they get along well together. There is no such thing as a happy family without a happy marriage.

(This is not to say, however, that if you are a single parent, for whatever reason, you are doomed to an unhappy family life. As I said in the introduction, the Holy Spirit will help any family, anytime, to become all that it can be, if parents put their trust in the Lord.) If you are a single parent, then God deals with you as an individual, and He has promised to fill that vacancy with His Holy Spirit.

Countless books have been written about marriage, and the authors suggest a variety of vital *keys* to a happy marriage. As important as all these keys may be, one of them—often neglected in the lists—takes precedence for Christians. It's what changed my own marriage and now forms the heart of this book. Very simply stated, it is the *filling of the Holy Spirit* (or the *control* or the *empowering* of the Holy Spirit—these phrases all mean the same thing). Without an ongoing, surrendered relationship with God in the power of His Spirit, you cannot achieve that taste of heaven in your family life.

In my husband's years of pastoral counseling, he conferred with several thousand couples who were in the throes of marital discord. The husband and wife may have started their marriage in the power of God's Spirit, but somehow they slipped away from living that way. Tim would point out the recent absence of divine assistance, only to hear one of them admit, "We used to live like that, and we didn't have these problems in those days." Eventually, he became convinced that the only kind of marital counseling that would bear fruit would be that in which the counseling concentrated on the Spirit-controlled life rather than on the symptoms and problems of troubled marriages.

This is a vital truth: If a husband and a wife walk in the Spirit, both of them can live with or resolve their problems. If they refuse to walk in the Spirit, all the counseling on problem areas and symptoms can be likened to a doctor putting a Band-Aid on a broken leg. The choice is clear: choose to walk in the Spirit, or, by default, walk in your human strength. The Bible tells us:

> Those who live according to the sinful nature have their minds set on what that nature desires; but those who live in accordance with the Spirit have their minds set on what the Spirit desires. The mind of sinful man is death, but the mind controlled by the Spirit is life and peace; the sinful mind is hostile to God. It does not submit to God's law, nor can it do so.
>
> —ROMANS 8:5–7, NIV

This is true for every believer, and therefore it is true for every married couple. Why, then, should we ever hesitate to be filled with the Holy Spirit?

> Therefore lift your drooping hands and strengthen your weak knees, and make straight paths for your feet, so that what is lame may not be put out of joint, but rather be healed.
> —Hebrews 12:12, rsv

Toward Success in Marriage

Of course, simply telling a troubled couple, "You need to be filled with the Holy Spirit," is too simplistic. In fact, they might reject your advice because it sounds like such a pat answer. We need to flesh out what it means. Here are four foundational requirements for finding marital happiness through the ministry of the Holy Spirit.

1. *You must be a Christian.* Only those who have invited Jesus Christ into their lives can be guided by His Holy Spirit. (See Romans 8:9–16.) The introduction of this book reminds us about God's invitation, and it summarizes what our response to the Father, Son, and Holy Spirit should be.

2. *Seek biblical instruction by regular Bible reading and study.* Become a sponge for the Word of God. Soak it up. Read your Bible, and avail yourself of Word-based resources such as other books, music, sermons, seminars, and the advice of trusted godly friends. The more familiar you become with God's Word, the easier it will be for you to differentiate His voice from the clamor of other voices in the world. The Bible is the primary way we can know God's will for our lives.

3. *Be willing to do the will of God no matter what it is.* Jesus said, "Blessed are those who hear the word of God and *keep* it!" (Luke 11:28, emphasis added). Merely calling yourself a Christian and even knowing the principles of the kingdom of God are not guarantees of happiness. That blessing is reserved for those who both know His will and obey Him. Pastors

spend their lifetimes counseling very miserable people, most of them Christians. Often, they have earned the right to be miserable by disobeying God. You cannot disobey God and expect to be happy. (Sometimes the pastors themselves don't know this, and therefore they cannot genuinely help others.)

4. *You must be filled with the Holy Spirit* (Eph. 5:18). The way of happiness for the Christian comes only in living life God's way—being obedient to God's principles. God's way is empowered by the Holy Spirit. Too many Christians know almost nothing about the Spirit-filled life and the immeasurable blessings it can provide for them, their family, and their interpersonal relationships. Some think of the filling of the Spirit as automatic, requiring no action on the part of the believer. Others think it is optional and that they can seek the filling of the Spirit if all else fails. In fact, the Holy Spirit is more than willing to empower and beautify your life if, by faith, you are willing to do His will.

THE FILLING OF THE HOLY SPIRIT

The reason many Christians are confused about the ministry of the Holy Spirit in their lives is that they tend to get their information from the experiences and opinions of other people rather than from the Bible. Besides confusion, this can bring them to an unnecessary fear of the power of the Spirit. Let's take a moment to look at our Lord's teaching about the Holy Spirit to His disciples in the sixteenth chapter of the Book of John.

Jesus' disciples were dismayed when they learned that He was going back to the Father. Jesus assured them, "It is to your advantage that I go away; for if I do not go away, the Helper will not come to you; but if I depart, I will send Him to you" (John 16:7). Jesus explained that the Helper (another name for the Holy Spirit) would bring conviction regarding "sin and righteousness and judgment." Then He said to them:

> I still have many things to say to you, but you cannot bear them now. However, when He, the Spirit of truth, has come, He will guide you into all truth; for He will not speak on His own authority, but whatever He hears He will speak; and He will tell you things to come.
>
> —JOHN 16:12–13

The Holy Spirit is the only member of the Godhead who is with us all the time, for He dwells within our hearts. He is the one who shows us when we are straying off the path, and He is our source of wisdom. Because He loves us with an everlasting love, He can get our attention by making us miserable when we are out of step with biblical principles. I believe that is why Tim and I got started off on the wrong track. We knew so little about how the Holy Spirit could change our attitudes and relationships. Although we both had been raised to love Jesus, had attended a Christian college, and believed it was important to attend church, the teaching of the work of the Holy Spirit in our lives was missing.

As I look back now on those beginning years, I realize how different the first years of our marriage could have been. I believe that is why I feel compelled to write this book—that young couples starting their life together can benefit from the errors of those who have gone before them. I pray that will be true.

ONE ESSENTIAL FOR CHRISTIAN LIFE

Success in the Christian life is completely impossible without the ministry of the Holy Spirit. He is our source of truth and assurance of salvation, and He leads us to glorify our Lord Jesus Christ in all that we do (John 16:7–15). We are so dependent on the Holy Spirit that we can't even pray properly without Him.

The Holy Spirit is not an optional extra in the life of a Christian. Christians are *commanded* to be filled with the Spirit (Gal. 5:16; Eph. 5:18). In obedience to the command, if for no other reason, we should invite the Spirit to fill our hearts. Each morning ask the Holy Spirit to fill you and guide you. God does not make His commands arduous, nor do we have to beg Him to permit us to do something He has already ordered us to do. We do have to meet His conditions, however, and the primary condition of being filled with the Spirit is to be a born-again Christian, as we have seen. Equally important to successfully becoming a Spirit-controlled Christian is complete surrender to God's will.

"How do we know God's will?" you ask. The best way to find out what it is in every aspect is to familiarize yourself with the Bible, as I have already mentioned. As you immerse yourself in the Word, which is a lifelong endeavor with eternal rewards, you will find yourself following these three steps over and over as you discover new aspects of your inner life.

1. *You will examine your life for sin and confess it.* "If we confess our sins, He is faithful and just to forgive us our sins and to cleanse us from all unrighteousness" (1 John 1:9.) The first characteristic of the Holy Spirit is *holiness*. Sinfulness is the opposite of holiness. God is holy, and He cannot tolerate sin; therefore, we cannot be filled with God's Holy Spirit and continue in sinful practices at the same time.

    We can expect to have "sin checks" throughout our lives. In a Communion service, we are challenged to examine ourselves for sin. "A man ought to examine himself before he eats of the bread and drinks of the cup" (1 Cor. 11:28, NIV). If we take time to examine our hearts, the Holy Spirit will "convict" us (trigger our conscience to recognize how we have transgressed against His love, thereby creating "good guilt" in us). Then we will know what we should repent of.

    When you find sin in your life, don't be surprised if that sin fits a habitual pattern of a "besetting" sin. All of us have a tendency to fall into sin habits. Because of our temperaments, backgrounds, and habits, we are vulnerable to falling in specific ways. The good news is that your sins can be forgiven—and re-forgiven many times. But no one can be controlled and empowered by the Spirit if he tenaciously clings to a sin habit that he is unwilling to forsake. In Psalm 66:18, the psalmist teaches us that if we harbor sin in our hearts, the Lord will not hear our prayer.

2. *You will surrender your will completely to God.* (See Romans 6:11–14.) Each time you repent of known sin and receive God's cleansing forgiveness, tell Him that you belong to Him 100 percent—that is, you are willing to do anything He instructs you to do.

I have learned to make my dedication more definite by visualizing myself lying on an Old Testament sacrificial altar, picturing myself as a voluntary sacrifice. I declare something like, "O Lord, I am fully yielded to Your control. I relinquish my mind, talents, family, vocation, money, and future. Use me as You wish, to Your glory."

Every time you surrender your will to God, be sure to include in particular whatever the Lord has been speaking to you regarding your fears, thoughts, or ambitions.

3. *You will ask to be controlled by the Holy Spirit.* Now that you are empty of the sin that competes with the holiness of God, simply ask Him to fill you once again. Think of it as putting a white robe of righteousness on your spirit. "Clothe yourselves with the Lord Jesus Christ, and do not think about how to gratify the desires of the sinful nature" (Rom. 13:14, NIV). Your robes of righteousness are like bridal garments, and holiness is a love gift from your Bridegroom, Jesus, to you.

So often we make the mistake of considering repentance and holiness as odious requirements of a legalistic God. Our tendency is to construct an artificial list of dos and don'ts. How much simpler and more freeing it is to simply relinquish whatever is blocking the love of God in our lives and to ask to be washed and restored to Him! A life that is filled, controlled, and empowered by the Holy Spirit is a love life of the highest order.

How often should you ask to be filled with the Holy Spirit? The answer is simple: ask whenever you think you are not.

If you realize you have grieved Him, tell Him that you are sorry, and ask Him to forgive you and to restore your fellowship with Him. When you wake up each morning, ask Him to fill you that day with His Holy Spirit. During the day, when you realize you have wandered off again, doing your own thing, come back to Him and ask Him to forgive you and to draw you near to Him. Ask for more of His love as you drift off to sleep at night. In time, asking for the Spirit's forgiveness and help will be as natural as breathing. I wish I could tell you that this is a rare prayer for me, but I must confess that my human side rises up once in a while, and I have to ask God to forgive me and to restore me, refilling me with the Holy Spirit.

Some teachers have made it so mysterious, so complex, and so theological that the average person can neither understand nor enjoy the Spirit-filled life. We also hear experience-oriented people who can tell their stories with such animation and excitement that their listeners feel rather inadequate by comparison, thinking, My *life is nowhere near that thrilling.*

To live a Spirit-filled and Spirit-empowered life means that you are living a life in *relationship* with God. You start where your situation is at any given time, and you present yourself to Him. It doesn't matter if you understand all of the theology, and it doesn't matter if your experience is dramatic. All that matters is that you relate to Him.

Nobody can be controlled by his or her own will *and* by the Holy Spirit at the same time. One or the other will predominate; either a person will act according to his old selfish nature, or he will act according to his or her Spirit-renewed nature. It is easy to tell the difference. When self is in control, a person will exhibit selfishness, anger, resentment, fear, or other "works of the flesh." If the Holy Spirit is in charge, the fruit of the Spirit will prevail.

15

The Fruit of the Spirit

"But the fruit of the Spirit is love, joy, peace, patience, kindness, goodness, faithfulness, gentleness and self-control" (Gal. 5:22–23, NIV). It is impossible for a Christian to be filled with the Holy Spirit and not evidence this filling in some manner. Examine this list, and you will find a quality sufficient to overcome every single weakness in your life. Nothing is more practical on a day-to-day basis than the control of our lives by God's Holy Spirit.

The fruit of the Spirit expresses the being and character of God. When we demonstrate the fruit of the Spirit, we are reflecting His image to those around us. His love makes our hearts glad, and we begin to treat the people around us as He would treat them. In addition, the fruit of His Spirit in us rebounds to bless the Lord Himself as we walk faithfully in humility—enjoying the ongoing relationship with Him that He desires.

When a natural human being is indwelt by the supernatural power of the Holy Spirit, that person will become different. He or she does not get better looking or smarter or more talented. The difference will be evident in that person's emotions. New Christians often talk about the noticeable change in their lives since they turned them over to the Lord. A good portion of this change is due to the work of the Holy Spirit on their emotions. The Holy Spirit provides us with emotional control that enables us to have control over our out-of-control tendencies.

By contrast, when you see a Christian out of emotional control, you know that person is not walking in the Spirit. We all know what that feels like. Often God uses us to help each other get back on track.

Just recently I had an experience like that. A Christian lady who has a very strong, dominant temperament was becoming very aggressive and was barking out orders. Her orders were in direct conflict with what seemed the obvious way to go. I'm afraid I grieved the Holy Spirit by my retort to her, and immediately I felt guilty. I'll admit I was very tired, but that is a lame excuse for my actions. My true desire is to please God and to be commended for living by faith, which was also Enoch's desire as we can see in Hebrews 11:5. I quickly confessed my lack of patience to God, and He gave me the wisdom to know how to handle this situation through the control of the Holy Spirit.

Our different temperaments make us vulnerable to particular temptations and sins, but every one of them can be overcome by the power and love of the Holy Spirit, especially if we are surrounded by family or friends who can remind us about how He wants to work in us.

When a person is filled with the Spirit, he or she will get better and better at maintaining emotional control, regardless of inbred personality traits. Do you have a problem with anger? As we will explore in more depth later in this book, anger is the number-one destroyer of marriage and family life. But it can be brought under control by the "love, joy, peace, patience, kindness, goodness, faithfulness, gentleness and self-control" of the Holy Spirit. The same is true for many of the other emotions that so easily get out of control in our lives. The final chapter of this book is entirely about how the fruit of the Spirit makes family life abundant.

In an earnest effort to behave in a godly way, people may attempt to display the fruit of the Spirit, behaving, for instance with extra-sweet gentleness or enthusiastic joy. But without the Holy Spirit, all such virtuous behavior is mere imitation. The fruit of the Spirit is what a person *is*, not what he or she *does*. Juicy apples characterize a healthy apple tree. The apples mature naturally on the boughs, and the fruit is renewed season after season. The apples are not some kind of realistic, plastic fruit. In the same way, the true fruit of the Spirit characterizes a truly Spirit-filled Christian who is being renewed season after season.

When your children, who are still immature, are out of emotional control, you as their Spirit-filled parents can capably guide them into increased maturity. One evening, a kindergartner was whining and showing off, disrupting the family and guests, and he wouldn't stop when his mother told him to. After taking him out of the room to discipline him, she said to her guests, "I find it hard to believe that being allowed to be poorly behaved now will somehow magically change with adulthood. A child who is selfish now will grow into a selfish adult." This young mother was helping her son to grow in his ability to lay hold of the fruit of the Spirit.

Learning to walk in the Spirit in a consistent way—that is the essence of Spirit-empowered family life:

> ...but, speaking the truth in love, may grow up in all things into Him who is the head—Christ—from whom the whole body, joined and knit together by what every joint supplies, according to the effective working by which every part does its share, causes growth of the body for the edifying of itself in love.
>
> —Ephesians 4:15–16

As a wife, do you think you could get excited about going to the door when your husband arrives home from work if you knew that you would be greeting a man who, in spite of the day's pressures and ordeals, is filled with love, joy, peace, patience, kindness, goodness, faithfulness, gentleness, and self-control? Instead of driving home wallowing in self-pity, nursing grudges, or resenting other drivers, he would have conquered his reactions to the events of the day with the help of the Spirit within him.

As a husband, do you think you could enjoy walking into your home at the end of a long workday if you knew that you would be greeted by a loving, happy, peaceful, patient, kind, good, faithful, gentle, and self-controlled wife? No matter how pressured with babies, her workload, crises, and interruptions, the Spirit-filled wife would have the spiritual resources that would make all the difference.

How would your children react if you were able, even when upset, to return quickly to being a stable, strong, and loving father or mother? What a testimony to your children this would be! The advice contained in Ephesians 5, which we will examine next, would be much easier to follow.

SPIRIT-FILLED FAMILY LIVING

Ephesians 5:17 through 6:4 contains the most extensive instruction on Spirit-filled family living to be found in the entire New Testament. Paul begins this portion of his letter to the Christians in Ephesus by stating his primary point:

> Therefore do not be unwise, but understand what the will of the Lord is. And do not be drunk with wine, in which is dissipation; but be filled with the Spirit.
>
> —EPHESIANS 5:17–18

This is the most specific command in the Bible about being filled with the Spirit. If we want to be wise and to understand God's will, we will pay attention to it. The comparison and the contrast are clear: instead of being filled with wine—that is to say, *drunk*, which implies that we have yielded control to the effects of alcohol—we are to be filled with and thereby controlled by the Spirit.

Interestingly, these verses immediately precede the most extensive instruction on family living to be found in the entire New Testament. (The chapter division does not break the flow of the passage; chapter divisions were added long after Paul wrote the letter.) Notice that the instruction does not concern so much the life of a church body or how a single Christian should spend his or her time as it does the day-to-day life of a Spirit-empowered *family*. Here is an outline of the passage:

⋆ 5:18—the command to be filled with the Spirit

⋆ 5:19–20—three results of the Spirit-controlled life: (a) praising God by singing together; (b) "making melody in your heart" to God; and (c) giving thanks to God in Jesus' name for everything in your life

❧ 5:22–24—the command for wives to submit to their husbands

❧ 5:25–33—the command for husbands to love their wives sacrificially

❧ 6:1–3—the command for children to obey their parents

❧ 6:4—the command for fathers to nurture their children

This passage of Scripture is a recipe for happy family life.

When, with the help of the Holy Spirit, the husband learns to love his wife "as Christ also loved the church, and gave himself for it" (Eph. 5:25, KJV), and when he "loves [his] own [wife] as [he loves his] own [body]" (v. 28), he sets the stage for her wholehearted, trusting submission. It is striking that the husband is admonished to achieve a more thorough expression of commitment than his wife is expected to demonstrate.

If, moreover, a husband who is also a father nurtures his children well, he makes it easy for his children to obey him and their mother: "Fathers, do not provoke your children to wrath, but bring them up in the training and admonition of the Lord" (Eph. 6:4). Note that this is addressed to the fathers, not to the mothers, who might be expected to nurture their children naturally.

A wife who submits to her husband, "as the church is subject to Christ" (Eph. 5:24), finds joy in surrendering her well-being to a godly man who reflects Jesus' love to her daily. Hers isn't a slavish, passive role, but an expression of her personal commitment to the Lord. When a wife resists this kind of submission, she is really resisting obeying and submitting her life to Jesus Christ.

If both parents carry out their daily duties with a cheerful attitude and rejoicing in all circumstances, they set an example for the children to do the same. (See Ephesians 5:19; 1 Thessalonians 5:16–18.) The Holy Spirit is invited into the home. The family members seek His help, together and individually. Whenever someone falters, the Spirit helps in whatever way is best. He informs their consciences when they have sinned, and He provides wisdom to do the will of God.

The Spirit-controlled family is altogether *real*, doing everything from car repair to vacations to diaper duty out of their God-given and God-redeemed personalities and gifts.

※　※　※　※　※

Everyone knows that the rubber meets the road *in our homes.* You can't fake being a Holy Spirit–empowered family. The first bump in the road will blow a tire!

Spiritual Power for Your Family: Prayer

Father God,

I want to be filled with Your Holy Spirit, and I want my spouse and my family to be filled with Your Spirit as well. I invite You to become the source of life and love for us.

Using the words of Paul as a prayer for my family, I ask on their behalf: "May the God of hope fill you with all joy and peace in believing, so that you may abound in hope by the power of the Holy Spirit" (Rom. 15:13). I declare with faith and joy: "As for me and my house, we will serve the Lord" (Josh. 24:15).

In the name of my Lord Jesus, amen.

CHAPTER 2

Your Family Walking in the Spirit

God not only commands believers to be filled with the Spirit (Eph. 5:18), but He also commands us to "walk" in the Spirit. Being filled with the Spirit is not the same thing as walking in the Spirit, which means living under the control of the Holy Spirit. "If we live in the Spirit, let us also walk in the Spirit" (Gal. 5:25). Being filled with the Spirit makes very little difference in our lives if we don't take an active part in drawing on the Spirit's power to grow to maturity in Christ.

Walking in the Spirit is an outgrowth of being filled with the Spirit, because you cannot walk in the Spirit until you are filled with the Spirit. Our walking makes us need more filling, and the filling enables us to walk in the Spirit more. This is akin to drinking as much water as you can hold, and then walking in the energy of that life-giving water. Eventually, you get dehydrated, and you need to drink more in order to have sufficient fluid to walk farther.

So walking in the Spirit requires regular refilling, and we need to develop new habits to ensure that we won't become passive about our spiritual life.

Food for Our Spirits: The Word of God

One of those new habits should be a daily practice of reading the Bible. The psalmist knew this to be true:

> Blessed [happy] is the man
>   who does not walk in the counsel of the wicked
> or stand in the way of sinners
>   or sit in the seat of mockers.
> But his delight is in the law of the LORD,
>   and on his law he meditates day and night.
> He is like a tree planted by streams of water,
>   which yields its fruit in season
> and whose leaf does not wither.
>   Whatever he does prospers.
>
> —PSALM 1:1–3, NIV

What's the best way to make sure that you and your family can become consistent in Bible reading? That question has a variety of answers, because individuals and their families are so different from each other.

Some people find it easy to develop a habit of sitting down at a particular time each day to pick up their Bibles and open them to where they put their bookmark the day before. Since I am an early riser, I find it best to read the Bible before 8 a.m. when the phone starts ringing and the interruptions begin. For others, especially those with demanding or irregular daily routines, those who tend to be more spontaneous, or those who have difficulty with reading in general, this is simply not an option—"been there, done that, and it just doesn't work for me." Instead of feeling badly about their inability to develop the habit of daily Bible reading, perhaps the best solution for these people is to listen to the Bible in recorded form while driving the car, jogging, or working around the house. In addition, they may enjoy listening to Scripture-based hymns and worship songs.

Songs that have words lifted straight from the pages of the Bible can be a marvelous help to memorizing Scripture. Scripture memorization is an important benefit of Scripture reading. In Psalm 119:11 we read, "I have hidden your word in my heart that I might not sin against you" (NIV). If we have the Word tucked into our hearts and minds, we don't need to have a Bible handy to be reminded of God's truth. There is no single way to best memorize Scripture, because people's learning styles are as different as their temperaments. Find what works for you, and you will never regret having made the effort to hide God's Word in your heart.

Perhaps this goes without saying, but I'll say it anyway: to encourage your own Bible reading and to increase your family's exposure to the Word, explore different translations of the Bible. So often people have given up on trying to read their Bibles, saying, "I just can't understand it!" You can go to a Christian bookstore and browse through the selection of Bibles, comparing the same passage of Scripture in each one. Choose a version that appeals to you, one that seems fresh and clear and new to your ear. Even the venerable King James Version has been revised—I have quoted it throughout this book.

If you haven't ever done so, you might decide to purchase a Bible with notes and helps included in it. Having some expert perspective and some clear explanations can make all the difference between routine page turning and a life-giving experience. Some Bibles also include reading plans to motivate you to read every day.

FAMILY BIBLE TIME

What about family Bible reading? Do you consider that to be an outdated tradition, or can it be resurrected to become a new practice for your own family?

If your children are young, perhaps you can read them a Bible story from a children's Bible every day. Possibly Dad can read aloud a short excerpt from an easy-to-comprehend version of the Bible at the dinner table, or Mom can pray biblical prayers over the children each evening when she puts them to bed, repeating the same scriptural phrasing until it enters into each child's spirit. For example: "Because Johnny loves You, Lord, I ask You to rescue him and protect him, for he trusts in Your name" (a short prayer based on Psalm 91:14). Some other possibilities of biblical prayer starters include Ephesians 1:3–4, Ephesians 3:14–21, and 1 Peter 1:3–8 from the New Testament, and Psalm 4:8, Psalm 25:4–7, Psalm 139:4–18, and Isaiah 25:1 from the Old Testament.

I know of one mother, who happened to possess a splendid singing voice, who sang Scripture-based songs for her young son every night when she put him to bed. When he requested that she sing *all* the verses of "Great Is Thy Faithfulness" for the third night in a row, she gladly postponed his bedtime to sing them for him. She knew he would never forget the words as he grew up.

As a teenager, my husband wanted to go to summer camp, but his single-parent mother could not afford the cost. However, the youth pastor had a contest for camp in which the young person who memorized the most Scripture could win the entire camp cost. The second-place winner had half of the camp fee paid. For five years in a row, Tim won either first or second place each year and was able to go to camp every year. But more important than going to camp was the amount of Scripture that he memorized. We have estimated that he memorized over eight hundred verses of Scripture. After high school, he went into the United States Air Force for two years, and I'm sure the many Scripture verses he had memorized helped to keep his life pure in the midst of temptation.

> I have hidden your word in my heart that I might not sin against you.
>
> —Psalm 119:11, NIV

Wise parents will make sure their children and young people experience some kind of organized Bible memorization. Many churches have opened their doors to the Awana program, which is a very helpful and effective Scripture memorization program for youth. I would encourage all parents to give this serious consideration.

Recently I spoke with a mother who told me about her teenage daughter, who was on the verge of yielding to a temptation that she knew was a sin. Just about the time she was ready to give in to the temptation, some of the verses she had memorized earlier in her life flashed across her mind, and it caused her to stop dead in her tracks. She was able to walk away and thank God for protecting her from a pitfall that could have been her destruction.

The next chapter is devoted entirely to the subject of family prayer. Family Bible reading fits naturally with family prayer times.

Often we hear Psalm 119:105 quoted: "Thy word is a lamp unto my feet, and a light unto my path" (KJV). The Word of God is to a person what gasoline is to a car. Without fuel, even the most expensive machine in the world will not operate. As essential as it is to eat regularly to give you the strength to walk physically, so it is essential to feed your mind and spirit on the living Word of God day by day to gain the spiritual strength to walk in the Spirit on a daily basis.

GUARD YOUR STEPS

We are told, "Live by the Spirit, and you will not gratify the desires of the sinful nature" (Gal. 5:16, NIV). Informed and renewed by the Word of God, our minds and spirits become increasingly sensitive to the presence of sin in our lives. Sin is extremely subtle and will keep you from walking in the Spirit.

What do I mean by *sin*? It's one of those words we use often without thinking, or one we may try to *avoid* using if we're unsure of its implications for our lives.

Sin has its origin in our *flesh*, our human hearts and wills, and it separates us from God. Defined broadly, *sin* is any thought or action that separates us from God. James, who was the brother of Jesus, teaches us that "anyone, then, who knows the good he ought to do and doesn't do it, sins" (James 4:17, NIV). We have been captured by our sin, and we are its prisoners. (See Acts 8:22–23.) Every single human being on the face of the earth is afflicted with sin.

> What shall we conclude then? Are we any better? Not at all! We have already made the charge that Jews and Gentiles alike are all under sin. As it is written: "There is no one righteous, not even one."
>
> —ROMANS 3:9–10, NIV

To enable us to be forgiven of our sin, Jesus came to earth to become the only human being who was ever sin-free and was crucified and resurrected from the dead. Then, because we continue to sin even if we believe in Jesus, God gave us His Holy Spirit to help us to overcome our sinful tendencies on a continuing basis. (See Romans 5:12–17; 6:2–4.)

Having sin in your life is like wearing ill-fitting walking shoes or having something rubbing your heel or toes while you're walking—before long, you will develop a limp. We need to pay attention to our spiritual walk. When we notice any tendency to limp or shuffle, we should ask the Holy Spirit to show us what to do about it. He will show us how to repent, and He will teach us how to walk better. It is a lifelong process with joyful rewards.

> Make straight paths for your feet, so that what is lame may not be dislocated, but rather be healed. Pursue peace with all people, and holiness, without which no one will see the Lord.
>
> —HEBREWS 12:13–14

"Be Ye Holy"

The Bible teaches us that God has called us to holiness. The goal of our Creator and Savior is for us to be remade into His holy image, to be men and women who can walk in righteousness.

In the Word we read, "Be ye holy; for I am holy" (1 Pet. 1:16, KJV; cf. Lev. 11:44–45.) In other words, God wants us to share in His holiness. But He knows, better than we do, that we cannot achieve any degree of true holiness in our own strength. Therefore He has provided His Spirit to enable us to grow and change so that we can reflect His purity.

Far from becoming sanctimonious, "holier-than-thou" Christians, we are meant to reflect His character increasingly, having been "set apart" (a basic component of the meaning of the word *holy*) for special purposes and special attention.

Turning from sin

The remedy for sin is not complicated. It consists of a sequence of four simple steps:

1. Recognize and identify sinful behavior.

2. Admit it to God, and ask forgiveness.

3. Repent of it. Repentance means turning your back on the sin and turning toward God.

4. Restoration, if necessary, to a person you may have hurt or wronged. For example, if a married Christian gets involved in an adulterous affair, but then recognizes that this is sinful behavior (which will happen unless the person is a deceived Christian), then he or she will admit the sin to God and ask for forgiveness. "If we confess our sins, He is faithful and just to forgive us our sins and to cleanse us from all unrighteousness" (1 John 1:9). After repentance, the sinner separates himself or herself from any temptation to go back and turns

29

toward God and His righteousness. The sinner makes restitution and restores the relationship with the spouse, who was wronged and hurt by the adultery.

With the help of the Holy Spirit, we can become increasingly sensitive to the presence of sin in our lives. With His help, we are able to repent quickly. We are also able to lean on the strength that God provides through His Spirit to change our ways.

Sounds simple enough. But of course we all know that our fleshly natures are stubborn and even blind to sin. We like our familiar ways, even if they result in confusion or lead us down dead ends. What do conviction of sin and repentance look like?

Perhaps you are a "worrier" mother. Maybe you also have a strong desire to acquire things. "Shop till you drop" is one of your mottoes, and another one is, "Worrying is part of my job description." These things just seem to be part of your personal makeup, and your family and others accept them as such, even treating them lightheartedly. Nobody has ever mentioned the word *sin* in conjunction with these things. *Weaknesses*, perhaps, but not *sin*. You realize vaguely that you could trust God for your provision, but you have no idea what that would feel like.

Then one day you are reading a devotional book, and you pray a little prayer based on Psalm 51:2: "Wash me thoroughly from my iniquity, and cleanse me from my sin." After you pray, you worry your way through another ordinary day and spend the evening poring over some new catalogs that came in the mail. Something about it doesn't seem the same, and you wonder vaguely what's different.

The next day, you run across Matthew 6 in your Bible:

> Therefore I tell you, do not worry about your life, what you will eat or drink; or about your body, what you will wear.... Who of you by worrying can add a single hour to his life? And why do you worry about clothes? See how the lilies of the field grow.... If that is how God clothes the

grass of the field...will he not much more clothe you, O you of little faith? So do not worry....For the pagans run after all these things, and your heavenly Father knows that you need them. But seek first his kingdom and his righteousness, and all these things will be given to you as well. Therefore do not worry about tomorrow, for tomorrow will worry about itself.

—MATTHEW 6:25, 27–28, 30–34, NIV

Suddenly, the blinders come off, and you feel a strange mixture of pain and joy. "This is *me!*" you realize. "I worry about my family and myself all the time, and I try to shop and accumulate as many possessions as I can for a kind of insurance against the future. Jesus is telling me not to worry about anything."

For the first time ever, you recognize that these patterns are the opposite of holiness, which can be summed up as simple trust in God's ever-present provision. The Holy Spirit gently reminds you of your prayer, and He also reminds you of another verse you heard someone quote recently: "There is no fear in love; but perfect love casts out fear" (1 John 4:18). On your knees, you tell the Lord you want Him to change you, that you're sorry for not trusting Him, that you realize you have substituted material things for His comfort, and that you have not allowed Him to be in control of the worrisome details of your life.

You pray something like this: "Father, forgive me for carrying on as if You aren't in my life. I see that it's sinful to worry, and it's sinful to try to provide for myself as if You can't do it. I'm sorry, and I want You to help me grow out of this way of living."

In 1 Peter 5:7, we read, "Cast all your anxiety on him because he cares for you" (NIV). When we know what He has promised us in His Word, we can cast our worries and anxieties on Him. When we learn to do this, we will be content, peaceful, even blithely unconcerned about the day ahead. Even if this level of peace doesn't last, you know that God will be helping you to overcome your old habits and thinking patterns. Your conscience has told you before when you have told a lie or spoken out of anger, but you never realized that the Holy Spirit's conviction of sin could apply to such things as worrying. And here you are, without a load of guilt or a feeling that you need to "shape up or else"—it's more like comfort and motivation to change, all rolled into one.

Sometimes later, God will allow a crisis to show you how much you have changed. If you have been praying for trust to replace your worry, you will be amazed to see how differently you react to an emergency. It worked—the Spirit's conviction and your response! From your heart, you will rejoice—and rejoicing is another distinctive of walking in the Spirit. (See Philippians 4:4–7.)

A HEAD START FOR YOUR CHILDREN

As parents "walk the walk" of holiness, their children learn how to do it in the best possible environment. Just as Dad and Mom are developing a keen sensitivity to sin, so will their children, especially as their parents provide the same kind of wise discipline for their children that the Holy Spirit provides for them. (See Hebrews 12:10–11.)

Although today's sin-saturated society makes a mockery of the ideals of righteous living, godly parents who model walking in the Spirit successfully give their children an invaluable head start in knowing right from wrong. Far more than absorbing opinions or memorizing rules of behavior, the children in a Spirit-controlled family can develop their own personal relationship with the Savior, whose Spirit is the most available Counselor in the world.

Now lest you get the wrong impression, I should make it clear that Spirit-empowered family members don't think about sin all the time. They just keep walking, enjoying their life together. Each day they listen to God and to each other, and they never stop growing in their love.

Clear direction

Besides victory over sinful tendencies, walking in the Spirit also means that we receive God's guidance for the daily decisions and choices we must make. Family members who are walking in the Spirit are alert to hear the "whispers" of His voice to direct them in both large and small matters. Much of His guidance occurs circumstantially, but some of it comes to us plainly, especially if we seek Him for it.

Often, the guidance of the Holy Spirit is very subtle, very much like a whisper in your ear. He may seem to push a quiet "pause" button in your spirit on a busy day, bringing your spouse, a child, or a friend to mind for whom He wants you to pray, or guiding you to take the time to write that letter to your congressman about a matter of moral concern. He wants to show you whether or not to take a new job, which piano teacher to choose for your daughter, or how to make arrangements for the care of your elderly parent.

This reminds me of the time my mother and my stepfather were past the age of being able to care for each other. My stepfather had lost his eyesight, and my mother was suffering with a heart ailment, so it was obvious that they needed extra care. Tim and I prayed about this with deep concern, because our home was too small to add them to our family living quarters. My sister and her husband were missionaries in Taiwan, so they could not take them in. I will not go into detail how the Lord worked this out, but we had the wonderful experience of watching the Lord take us step by step and provide us with a bigger home with an attached apartment that was just perfect for my elderly parents. God provided and answered our prayers in a way that we never dreamed was possible.

If we truly desire to follow the Lord as completely as possible, He will lead us to make prudent decisions, and He will help us accomplish great things in His kingdom. What an exciting way to live!

The Gifts of the Spirit

No discussion of walking in the Spirit would be complete without talking about the gifts of the Holy Spirit. As Spirit-filled family members live together in love and harmony in their home, they will be able to identify their spiritual gifts and how they can work together to help each other for good.

When we are Spirit-filled believers, we will begin to recognize which spiritual gifts God has given to us. (See Romans 12:6–8.) These gifts range all the way from serving and giving to leadership and pastoring. There are many books and commentaries that can help you understand the far-reaching possibilities of these gifts, although for most of us, what we know about our own gifts comes from firsthand experience. Our families are some of the best laboratories for life experience.

Spiritual gifts are not the same as the talents we were born with, although our Creator God has given both to us. The apostle Paul, who is an example of a man with a gift of apostolic leadership, said he had hardly any talent for speaking in public and that his physical presence was not impressive. (See 2 Corinthians 10:10.) A person's knack for writing well is a talent, not a spiritual gift, although it may be used to express a spiritual gift of teaching.

Spiritual gifts enable family members to serve each other and to serve outside the family in a way that demonstrates the grace of God in action. The apostle Peter advises believers:

> Each one should use whatever gift he has received to serve others, faithfully administering God's grace in its various forms. If anyone speaks, he should do it as one speaking the very words of God. If anyone serves, he should do it with the strength God provides, so that in all things God may be praised through Jesus Christ.
> —1 Peter 4:10–11, NIV

Before we move on, let me point out the warning from verse 11. Note that it says, "If anyone speaks, he should do it as one speaking the very words of God." The New King James Version reads: "If anyone speaks, let him speak as the oracles of God" (or the utterances of God). I cannot pass this verse without underlining how careful we must be when we are speaking, always glorifying the Lord Jesus Christ and speaking His truth.

Whether we are talking about talents or spiritual gifts, it is true that we feel happy and fulfilled when we use one of them. The activity flows naturally. It is not a struggle or a chore to do something for which we are gifted. Conversely, it may be quite difficult to try to do something for which we are not well equipped. To help each other, parents sometimes may decide to swap certain responsibilities to make them better match with their gifts. For instance, a dad who struggles to put together a little once-a-week Bible study for his family's devotional time may not have a gift of teaching. However, his wife may have that gift. One way to find out would be for her to try her hand at preparing a lesson. If she enjoys the process of preparing and presenting the material, the whole family can benefit from her efforts. (If neither of them seems to have this gift, they could locate some good study materials prepared by a person who does have the gift of teaching.)

By paying attention to children's developing spiritual gifts, parents can help their children decide about their future education and career direction. In addition, both spiritual gifts and God-given talents can underwrite family outreaches. If one or both parents are gifted in a particular way, the entire family can blend their gifts and efforts to achieve, for example, effective and merciful service to other families who are struggling with housing problems or meager finances. Some families have what seems to be a gift of hospitality, and their home becomes a welcome oasis for others. Other families collaborate to reach out with the gospel message or to organize valuable community initiatives.

Walking in the Spirit means walking in God's love, which in turn means that we will give His love away to others—quite often by means of our spiritual gifts. Without love, any spiritual gift is devoid of meaning. Remember the well-known words of 1 Corinthians 13:1: "Though I speak with the tongues of men and of angels, but have not love, I have become sounding brass or a clanging cymbal." This beautiful chapter leads us back full circle to the beginning of the next chapter: "Pursue love, and desire spiritual gifts" (1 Cor. 14:1). It's part of walking in the Spirit.

DO NOT QUENCH THE SPIRIT

To help us walk in the Spirit, another familiar portion of Scripture advises Christians, "Rejoice always, pray without ceasing, in everything give thanks; for this is the will of God in Christ Jesus for you. Do not quench the Spirit" (1 Thess. 5:16–19). Paul also wrote a similar directive to the church in Ephesus: "Do not grieve the Holy Spirit of God, by whom you were sealed for the day of redemption" (Eph. 4:30).

To state the obvious—you and your family cannot hope to keep walking in the Spirit if you quench or grieve the Spirit. What does it mean to do that? Let's explore the verses surrounding this essential warning, many of which concern our relationships with others.

Just before he wrote, "Do not quench the Spirit," in his letter to the Thessalonians, Paul had already spoken against idle loafing (1 Thess. 5:14, NIV), not being vindictive or contentious (v. 15), and respecting those in authority (vv. 12–13). He went on: "Do not despise prophecies. Test all things; hold fast what is good. Abstain from every form of evil" (vv. 20–22). Paul wants no one to quench the Spirit's fire because of sluggishness, a negative attitude toward people or God, or wrongdoing.

Not all of the safeguards against quenching the Spirit are negative, however. Paul also tells his readers that the best way to avoid quenching the Holy Spirit is to engage in all the positive conduct that he goes on to describe in the neighboring verses. The surest protection, he says, is to pursue righteousness. We learn more about what that means when we read the two verses after Ephesians 4:30: "Let all bitterness, wrath, anger, clamor, and evil speaking be put away from you, with all malice. And be kind to one another, tenderhearted, forgiving one another, even as God in Christ forgave you" (vv. 31–32). Scattered throughout the entire chapter, we find gems of wisdom for maintaining the peace and joy of family life in the Spirit. For example: "[Bear] with one another in love" (v. 2, NIV); "[Put] away lying" (v. 25); "Be angry, and do not sin" (v. 26); and "Let no corrupt word proceed out of your mouth, but what is good for necessary edification, that it may impart grace to the hearers" (v. 29).

Paul had already advised the people, "Rejoice always, pray without ceasing, in everything give thanks" (1 Thess. 5:16–18). These three simple phrases cover a lot of territory. *Always* praise the Lord, continually, regardless of circumstances or season of life. Pray to God *without ceasing,* not ever taking a vacation from talking with your Lord, acknowledging with gratitude that He is the Lord of all your life, of *everything,* even the hardships and discomforts.

Paul's advice seems like an instruction manual for successful family life in the power of the Holy Spirit, doesn't it? What family has not been a proving ground for the character development of its members, complete with emotional ups and downs, dishonesty, laziness, impatience, and disrespect? I have expanded upon these verses later in this book, because they are so important to understand and apply in our family life.

In short, to keep walking in the Spirit, you must…keep walking in the Spirit! As a family, help each other to listen to His whispers, to respond to His conviction of sin, to repent, to forgive, and to love.

❊ ❊ ❊ ❊ ❊

The power of the Holy Spirit will enable your family to rejoice always, and we "plug in to" the Spirit's enabling power by praying. In the next chapter, we will explore the adventure of prayer in a Spirit-controlled family.

SPIRITUAL POWER FOR YOUR FAMILY: PRAYER

Father God,

You are the Father of all families. I come before You now with one request: help my family to walk in the Spirit. I want my family to be obedient to Your instruction and responsive to Your voice.

Your ways are not the same as our ways, and we will need Your help to remember the difference. It's too easy for us to slip back into old patterns. Please trigger our consciences when we have strayed, and please show us the way out of troubles.

I thank You for all the ways in which You have shown us Your tender mercy and steadfast love. Together with the members of my family, I look forward to a future that is under Your direction.

In the name of Jesus, amen.

CHAPTER 3

The Power of Praying Parents

No PARENT HAS ever been perfect. Tim and I certainly weren't! If we had our parenting days to live over, we would do so many things differently. We wish we could say that when we were filled with the Holy Spirit, we became ideal parents, but God and our children know better. Without a doubt, we are much improved. But we were never perfect.

Fortunately, God doesn't expect perfection, and neither do your children. The Bible teaches, "All have sinned and fall short of the glory of God" (Rom. 3:23). That includes Christian parents. Spirit-filled Christians are not robots, and we still struggle with our old sin nature even as we walk in the Spirit.

Provision for Parents

A weeping mother stopped me after a seminar and sobbed, "Is there any hope for a parent who has done everything wrong!"

"Of course!" I replied. Why? As Christians, we have hope because we have a resource that is not available to non-Christians—*the power of prayer*. We are privileged to address the supreme, omnipotent Creator of all things as "Dear heavenly Father," for we have been adopted into the family of God. He has made us His children, and He wants us to converse with Him in prayer.

Jesus reassured us of the Father's interest in our prayers when He said, "If you then, being evil, know how to give good gifts to your children, how much more will your Father who is in heaven give good things to those who ask Him!" (Matt. 7:11). Just look at this sampling of scriptures that contain further words about prayer spoken by Jesus:

> Ask, and it will be given to you; seek, and you will find; knock, and it will be opened to you. For everyone who asks receives, and he who seeks finds, and to him who knocks it will be opened.
> —Matthew 7:7–8

> Whatever things you ask in prayer, believing, you will receive.
> —Matthew 21:22

> Ask, and you will receive, that your joy may be full.
> —John 16:24

> Men always ought to pray and not lose heart.
> —Luke 18:1

Jesus' words provide plenty of direction, but there is more. Throughout the Bible, many others portray prayer as their foundation:

The prayer of the upright is His [God's] delight.
—PROVERBS 15:8

Pray without ceasing.
—1 THESSALONIANS 5:17

In everything by prayer and supplication, with thanksgiving, let your requests be made known to God.
—PHILIPPIANS 4:6

The effective, fervent prayer of a righteous man avails much.
—JAMES 5:16

Prayer is to a family what a roof is to a house; it protects those within from the adversities of life. In many cases, it even protects the family members from themselves. I'm thinking of the woman who confided to me that while she was praying one morning, she sensed that her husband had been unfaithful. He had so carefully shielded himself from detection that she didn't have one clue of what he was doing. Going only on the strength of her prayerful sense, she quietly faced him with his sin. He was so flabbergasted that he blurted out, "How did you know?" Her early detection and confrontation resulted in his repentance, and they have enjoyed years of happiness as a result.

All dedicated parents utilize prayer power on behalf of their children at some time in their lives, particularly at times of great crisis. I vividly recall standing with Tim at the bedside of our five-year-old daughter Lori when she had her second bout with pneumonia. Her little chest was heaving as she gasped for every breath under the oxygen tent. The doctor said to Tim, "Preacher, if you've ever prayed in your life, you had better do it now. I've done all I can do. It is entirely up to God." I wept as Tim prayed, and God gave us a supernatural peace that Lori would get well. In a matter of minutes, she passed the crisis, and gradually the power of God restored her health.

Almost all families face crises like this at some time during the growing-up years of their children. Because we have a Savior, we have Someone real to turn to at such times. Frankly, I don't know how non-Christians make it.

PROVISION FOR CHILDREN

Most of us who are Christians today are the answer to someone else's prayers, often the prayers of our parents or grandparents.

Tim tells how the prayers of his mother redirected his steps after he returned home from military service. One day he came home to her apartment in the wee hours of the morning, and he found his mother kneeling at the couch, sound asleep. The living room was so small that he literally had to step across the back of her legs to get to his bedroom. At first it made him mad, because he knew she had stayed up praying for him, but after he got into bed, he couldn't sleep. He knew that she had stayed up late praying for him even though she had to get up for work at 5:30 a.m., so he went out and woke her up so she could spend the rest of the night in her own bed. But the scene haunted him for days until he finally decided to drop his application to a prelaw school and to go to a Christian university, where his life was transformed.

What kind of a world would this be if every young man had that kind of a praying mother? Prayer won't make up for a lifetime of parental mistakes, but it can result in life-changing miracles.

In some of these cases, prayer is like a court of last appeals. A teenager may have grown so tired of hearing her parent's sermons that she seems to become hardened to the things of the Lord. But prayer is not restricted by our human limitations or the intricacies of the situation. Through a parent's faith-filled prayer, God can soften the hardest heart. He often brings other godly men and women into children's lives when they refuse to listen to their parents any longer.

He can and does send life-directing experiences to our children as if they have been special ordered. (They have!)

GROWING IN PRAYER

You cannot walk in the Spirit without prayer. Prayer connects you with the source of all strength and wisdom, and His fortification transforms your life.

How easy it is to forget this truth! We get *too busy* and distracted. Prayer seems like a dispensable commodity, a nonurgent priority. Certainly the world around us does not model a life of prayer. Or we *think* we're praying when we engage in one of the following substitutes.

Prayer "clichés"

These are standard little phrases that are so over-used as to be nearly empty of personal meaning. For example:

- "God bless America."
- "God bless our home."
- "God bless us every one."
- "Now I lay me down to sleep..."
- "Bless this food to the use of our bodies."
- "Bless the missionaries all over the world."

Sad to say, many people never move beyond these rote statements. Prayer clichés aren't specific. They don't demonstrate a true understanding of what is at stake, nor do they involve any faith that God will answer. They are impersonal, and therefore they are largely ineffectual. If this is where you are, it's time to move beyond the stock phrases and learn how to hold a real conversation with your heavenly Father.

Instead of praying, "God bless America," you can ask yourself, "What exactly is it I want God to do for our country?" Are you concerned about America's attitude toward the pornography sweeping our country? Do you want America to help protect the lives of unborn babies? Should we pray for America's safety from terrorist assault? Can we ask God to bless America when we are turning our backs on God as a nation? Let's be on our knees praying very specifically about our concerns for America.

Impersonal information

Our Lord knows all things about us, but it is never wrong to be specific in making our requests to the Lord. He is never surprised with the little information we pray about, and I believe He desires to hear us express it to Him.

Be careful that your prayers do not develop into a horizontal communication between two human beings instead of being directed toward an omnipotent, omniscient God, the One who loves you and is able to answer your prayers. How much better it is to pray vertically—upward to your heavenly Father whose strength and power are great enough to raise the dead, who really wants to supply all your needs.

Giving your opinions to God

Too many people spend the majority of their prayer time telling God what He needs to do, when He needs to do it, and how it can be done. How incredibly presumptuous!

Instead, we need to present ourselves before the Lord with humble confidence that He has had our best interests in mind from the beginning. He can sort through all the complications to help us, and others, in the right way and at the right time.

◆ ◆ ◆ ◆ ◆

How much better it is to move past these elementary kinds of prayers and to graduate to new levels of maturity in our relationship with God. Each stage is more personal than the one before, and each brings us greater intimacy with our Father.

Sharing with God

When sin came into the world through Adam and Eve, the worst result was the separation it created between God and the ones He had created to be with Him. Our prayer is meant to bridge that separation, to move us back into a position of real intimacy with the God who loves us.

We move away from talking with God in a *religious* way when we begin to talk with Him as we would with our dearest personal friend, sharing with Him our dreams, our fears, and our emotional distresses.

In addition, we tell Him how we feel about Him—about our growing love for Him, our ongoing need for His forgiveness, and our appreciation for the large and small ways that He shows us that He cares.

Praying for loved ones

The better you get to know the Lord through your conversations with Him, the more natural it seems to bring others' needs to His throne. This is called *intercessory prayer* because we *intercede* on behalf of others, standing before God where they may or may not be able to stand on their own. This is a more strenuous level of prayer, yet anyone can achieve it.

Epaphras was one of Paul's friends, and he had a reputation for interceding for others: "Epaphras, who is one of you...greets you, always laboring fervently for you in prayers, that you may stand perfect and complete in all the will of God" (Col. 4:12). I thank God for the people who "labor fervently" for me in prayer that I might stand perfect and complete in the will of God. It is quite likely that I would miss the mark without their prayers. For my part, I intercede earnestly for my family and friends, for matters of concern in church and state, and for projects large and small.

Intercessory prayer becomes second nature to a believer who is in touch with God every day. With Holy Spirit–aided practice, we can *tune in* to God well enough to sense what He has on His heart. Then, full of confidence that He is praying through us, we can pray the most effective prayers, praying God's will back to Him.

> The Spirit helps us in our weakness. We do not know what we ought to pray for, but the Spirit himself intercedes for us with groans that words cannot express. And

he who searches our hearts knows the mind of the Spirit, because the Spirit intercedes for the saints in accordance with God's will.

—Romans 8:26–27, NIV

The Power of Prayer

In case you have ever wondered if prayer works, I'm here to tell you that everything I'm doing today is a tribute to the power of prayer. Let me tell you about it.

More than thirty years ago, I was in a minor automobile accident in which my arm was pulled out of its socket. It slipped right back in after a few minutes of excruciating pain, but overnight I was stricken with rheumatoid arthritis. From that day on, the crippling disease grew worse and worse. Since the day of that accident, I've hardly been without pain.

About two or three years after its onset, the arthritis was becoming quite severe. I couldn't hold a pencil in my hand. I couldn't write a letter or sign my name on a check. I was still a young woman. I had children and a husband who needed me. I went to Scripps Clinic near our home in San Diego for two weeks of testing. The doctors' report was not encouraging. They said I should take more than a dozen aspirin each day and that within the next couple of years I would probably be confined to a wheelchair.

Depression overwhelmed me. I tried hard to deny that my condition would really deteriorate so far, but I only had to look at my increasingly deformed hands and curled toes to see what was happening. I began to attend classes to relearn how to do ordinary tasks. I learned how to use my claw-shaped hands to pick up a cup. Doorknobs were especially difficult. I felt I was being programmed to be a cripple, but I didn't see that I had a choice in the matter.

This was surely the lowest period of my life; I call it my *black year*. Pain racked my body from head to toe. I tried every kind of treatment possible, but only a few of them brought me a measure of relief. Every morning, I awoke to find that a different part of me wouldn't work right. Instead of caring for my family, my husband and children were now caring for me. My depression and frustration were so deep that I couldn't even pray.

But Tim had more faith than I had. He took over praying for me when I couldn't pray for myself. Day after day, week after week, month after month, Tim spent hours pleading with God on my behalf. He wouldn't give up. He kept praying, he kept encouraging me, and he kept searching for an answer. He enlisted others to pray for me, all across the country.

And something began to happen. God led me to just the right doctors who could prescribe for me the right treatment and medication, and today I have a few days of minor pain, but nothing like I had before. My great fear was that I would be so crippled that I could not actively serve the Lord as my heart yearned to do. But God had other plans.

He has blessed me abundantly, and now I can pray for others again, and I can pray for myself as well. Many of my prayers are prayers of thanksgiving; although I have not seen an end to my disease, I have seen a miraculous answer to prayer! God does answer prayer! He enables us to do above and beyond anything that we could ask or think.

In fact, during those early years, God laid on my heart a heavy burden regarding the rapid decline of the family. I became concerned with how our culture was changing the God-given plan for the family. So a group of ladies joined me, and we started an organization called *Concerned Women for America* (CWA), created for the thousands of people who are also concerned about the moral decay surrounding the family and our children and grandchildren. Today you would call us a Christian pro-family lobbying group that has grown from nothing to over half a million women and many men. I am amazed at how God has blessed this organization to be effective in alerting Christian men and women to the dangers around us and what we can do to try to stop the evil that affects our families.

I sincerely believe the measure of CWA's success has been because of the CWA Prayer Chapters that have been built in every state and in many cities. There are hundreds of chapters led by godly women, and even some men, who meet on a monthly basis to pray for their families and their elected officials. Many of them also use this time to write letters to their congressmen to express their views and concerns.

Freedom From Fear

I am grateful for my physical healing, and I am equally grateful to have been delivered from debilitating fears. Again, prayer was the key.

One day in the early days of our ministry, my husband announced that he wanted to take flying lessons. In horror, I said, "You mean you want to fly an airplane with only *one engine?*"

"Yes," he said, "that's what I'd be starting off with. What do you think?"

Well, I didn't like the idea at all. "What if something goes wrong with the one engine? You won't have a spare!"

Tim asked me to pray about it. I did, telling God my opinion over and over: "Lord, You know how foolish this flying thing is. It's just too dangerous. Please change Tim's mind. Take away his desire to fly."

Tim was patient. But one day he said to me, "Honey, I know you've been praying about the flying lessons. I wonder, have you asked God to perhaps change *your* attitude?" That took me aback. "Be open with the Lord," Tim said. "Tell Him you're scared to death, but that you're willing to be changed if He wants to do that."

I followed his advice. Before long he was taking the lessons. After he had logged enough flying time, he invited me to go up with him for the first time. I went—praying every inch of the way. Much to my astonishment, as we took off, it suddenly became a spiritual experience. Just my husband and me in that little craft high up in the air, supported by God's loving arms underneath. After all my doubting and pleading, I found myself actually enjoying the flight. Forced to face my fears, I had learned to trust God to lift me above them.

I had no idea that God would later take us into areas of the world where we would have to fly in just such a plane, often under unsafe conditions. And many years later, Tim and I were passengers on a little commuter plane, accompanied by an attorney friend, when a turbulent storm blew up. The sky grew dark and ominous, and that little aircraft bounced around wildly. The attorney is not normally a fearful man, but he was terrified that day. He told me later that he began confessing every sin he had ever committed, and then he begged God to take care of his wife and family after he was gone. When he finished praying, he glanced over at us. Tim was busily writing away, and I was sound asleep.

"I don't get it," he told me later. "How could you sleep so peacefully?"

"It has to be God." I replied. "Only He could have brought me from my crippling fearfulness to such peace that I could sleep through a storm like that. Prayer was my weapon against fear, and it worked."

DAILY PRAYER

Need I ask you whether or not God answers prayer? Even if you have not experienced it yourself, I hope you will take my word for it—and begin your own prayer adventure with God. Far from being only a *last resort*, it's a never-ending journey that leads us straight to heaven as we press on every day.

Pray without ceasing

It may be a daunting prospect to "pray without ceasing" (1 Thess. 5:17), but it shouldn't be any more daunting than it is to breathe in and out many times a minute, whether we're awake or asleep. To get ourselves oriented, we only need to exercise a little Holy Spirit–inspired willpower to develop a habit of praying daily.

Whether or not you are a morning person as I am, do consider giving your attention to God in the first moments of your day. It's a routine well worth developing. I have found that I have a daily decision: I can wake up and start worrying about my busy schedule, which will cause the day ahead to be a hectic one, or I can turn to God first thing in the morning and ask Him to direct my day and give Him thanks for His blessings.

Often with worship music playing in the background, I commit my calendar and my concerns to Him. Resisting the urge to jump into a shopping list of requests, I have learned to pause to simply praise Him. When I start the day by letting the Holy Spirit direct my attention beyond my personal concerns, it seems that my prayers flow ceaselessly from then on as I get ready to go out the door or begin my tasks around our home. Believe me, there's a definite difference when occasionally I skip over my prayer time and spend the day operating under my own wisdom and strength.

Pray Scripture

God delights to hear His own Word in our conversations with Him. When you are praising Him with an open Bible (or a devotional book based on it), you will find an almost unlimited variety of ways to express your love to God. Praying straight from Scripture ensures that you are praying within His will for a situation.

Are you worried today? Pray, "Father, I cast all of my cares on You, because I know You care for me." (See 1 Peter 5:7.) Need strength and courage? Talk to Him about it: "You are a shield around me, Lord. You give me rest in sleep, and You lift me up and sustain me when I wake again. Because I trust You, I don't have to fear even tens of thousands against me on every side. You bring deliverance and blessing to me." (See Psalm 3:1–6, 8.)

Are you troubled and confused? "Lord, I know that Your thoughts are not the same as my thoughts. Mine are confused, but Yours are not. Your thoughts are as much better than mine as the heavens are higher than the earth." (See Isaiah 55:8–9.) "One thing I'm sure of—You have not given me a spirit of fear, but of power, love, and a sound mind." (See 2 Timothy 1:7). Or are you bursting with a song of praise that is beyond your capabilities to express? So was the ancient psalmist. With him you can pray: "I praise the Lord from the heavens. Praise Him, all His angels. Praise Him, sun and moon and stars! Praise Him, all you wild animals, all birds and fishes, all mountains and hills, all fruit trees, all kings and rulers, young men and women, old men and children." (See Psalm 148.)

Pray specifically

Even when you are using Scripture in your prayers, don't be too general. At least one good reason to be specific is that otherwise you won't know when God has answered your prayers. Specific prayers get specific results.

Many good examples have arisen over the years as CWA attorneys defend Christians in courtrooms. One time, there was an ice storm going on, and important witnesses were delayed. The judge was unsympathetic, even hostile. "If they can't get here, that's your problem. I'm here, and if they aren't, it's just too bad." The defendant and her CWA attorneys went to a hotel room and prayed, "Lord, please stop this trial. Please give us more time."

The next day, they received a phone call. Court was canceled. Two jury members had been injured on the way home, and the judge himself had to have emergency surgery. All three were in the hospital. While that's not what they prayed for, they had prayed specifically, and they got exactly what they prayed for. The trial didn't resume for four months.

Pray strenuously

I had observed that James 5:17 gives the example of Elijah praying "earnestly." Then one day I noticed that Luke 22:44 refers to *more earnestly* praying. I started wondering just what *more earnestly* meant. I looked it up in the Greek commentary, and I found that "earnestly" implies praying with fervor. How can you have more fervent fervor? So I looked up the Greek definition of the term in Luke and read, "To be stretched out or to strenuously pray, to pray exhaustively."

Sure enough, Luke 22:44 is referring to Jesus praying in the Garden

SPIRITUAL POWER FOR YOUR FAMILY

of Gethsemane, praying so strenuously that He sweat drops of blood.

What would it take for us as Christians to stretch ourselves in prayer to such a degree? If we are to pray as Jesus did, we need to learn more about exhausting ourselves when we pray.

Pray often

I believe that we ought to pray and pray and pray some more. Even though I am confident that God is not deaf, I am convinced that there is power in repetitive prayer.

Remember the story of the persistent widow in Luke's Gospel?

> [Jesus] said: "In a certain town there was a judge who neither feared God nor cared about men. And there was a widow in that town who kept coming to him with the plea, 'Grant me justice against my adversary.' For some time he refused. But finally he said to himself, 'Even though I don't fear God or care about men, yet because this widow keeps bothering me, I will see that she gets justice, so that she won't eventually wear me out with her coming!'"
> —LUKE 18:2–5, NIV

If the judge had responded to her request on the first day, she would have stopped coming back. As it was, she probably lost count of the number of days she returned with the same request to the same judge.

How did she know when to stop returning? How do you know when to stop praying? When you have received an answer or you go home to be with Jesus! We have all heard stories about persistent prayers for someone's salvation, prayers that were not answered until some time after the one who prayed had died—but they *were* answered.

Experience has taught me the importance of interceding persistently. We have one grandson who was born with a hearing deficiency, a chest that didn't fully develop, and jawbones that failed to grow properly. It was obvious that his serious problems would require a divine miracle. Through multiple surgeries, some with severe complications, doctors took ribs to extend his jaw and create two joints. There were times when he balanced between life and death. His parents and grandparents prayed and prayed and prayed some more. God heard and answered our many prayers! He is now a young man, and no one would ever guess that he has gone through such severe problems. He is a licensed helicopter pilot, and God is using him in a wonderful way. His desire is to become a "search and rescue" pilot.

As parents, intercede for your children every day, not only for your babies and toddlers but also especially for your older children, who have so many negative influences around them. Don't ever stop praying if you happen to have a "prodigal." (In chapter nine, "Leading Your Children to Christ," you will find more about prodigals.)

Pray as a couple

Tim and I prayed for our children, but when they approached their early teens years, we began to pray in earnest. That's when we suddenly realized that we *had* to get closer to God. We had always believed in prayer, and as individuals we had always prayed every day. But we had never established a daily habit of praying *together*, uniting our prayers as we had united our lives.

I remember when we started. On the first night Tim led in prayer about one specific concern he had on his heart. He prayed a brief prayer about it, and then I prayed about his concern. Next, Tim prayed about his second concern, and I prayed about that concern. He led all the concerns that night, and I followed him on each one, praying specifically for six or seven items on his prayer list.

The second night was my turn to lead. One by one, I prayed for several items on my list of prayer concerns, and each time Tim followed with a prayer of his own. The third night, Tim led our prayer again. Then I took another turn. After about two weeks of praying this way, we could no longer tell our concerns apart; the two had become one. We broadened our scope to include thanksgiving for prayers answered and expressions of trust in God's provision.

Like most couples, we have had to overcome some barriers to

praying together. Our prayers become somewhat *dry* periodically. Sometimes one of us has been sick or unable to participate fully. Often, our routine gets interrupted. But praying as a couple has become such a permanent part of our relationship that we don't get off the track for very long.

Praying together as a couple, besides enabling us to agree with each other in prayer, has turned out to be a form of "marriage insurance." We have discovered that we cannot pray together when we have unresolved anger or disharmony between us. Praying together takes away our desire to get even with each other (or with people outside our marriage), and it increases our desire to live a godly life together.

I can promise you that if you and your spouse begin to pray together, you will never regret it. If you are reluctant to begin, let your first prayer together be simple like a child's prayer: "Lord, teach us to pray as a couple. We don't know how." He will hear you, and He will answer.

✦   ✦   ✦   ✦   ✦

As one parent to another, I pray the following scriptural prayer for you, suggesting that, in turn, you also pray it for your spouse and for others. I urge you to always keep praying as the Holy Spirit Himself directs you, bringing everything before Him, from your desperation to your thanksgiving. (See Ephesians 6:18.)

SPIRITUAL POWER FOR YOUR FAMILY: PRAYER

For this reason I bow my knees to the Father of our Lord Jesus Christ, from whom the whole family in heaven and earth is named, that He would grant you, according to the riches of His glory, to be strengthened with might through His Spirit in the inner man, that Christ may dwell in your hearts through faith; that you, being rooted and grounded in love, may be able to comprehend with all the saints what is the width and length and depth and height—to know the love of Christ which passes knowledge; that you may be filled with all the fullness of God.

Now to Him who is able to do exceedingly abundantly above all that we ask or think, according to the power that works in us, to Him be glory in the church by Christ Jesus to all generations, forever and ever. Amen. (See Ephesians 3:14–21.)

CHAPTER 4

The Power of Family Prayer

P RAYING TOGETHER AS a family comes fairly naturally if a husband and wife have become "pray-ers" before children come along. Even if your family consists right now of only you and your spouse and an infant who is too young to talk, you can benefit from a regular family prayer time of some kind.

It will be easier to keep family prayer going if you make it part of your children's lives from their earliest years. However, even older families can establish some kind of family prayer together.

MEALTIME GRACE

Let's start by talking about praying before meals, because that is the only prayer that many families share. As one of the most consistent times in a day when a family is together, mealtime turns out to be a natural time for a family to pray together.

Mealtime *grace* or *the blessing* is a time of lifting up the name of God, a daily reminder that He is our Lord. When grace is said, everyone around the table is reminded of God's faithful provision. We're not thanking Him as much for the food as we're thanking Him for being our provider.

Who says the grace at your house? Dad? Mom? Everybody in unison? Some families take turns. Other families sing a short song together.

Do you *mean it* when you say grace? It is sometimes hard to pray the same memorized words every time with meaning, although any prayers can be valuable if they acknowledge God's lordship over your family life. For example, these well-known words, though used repeatedly, can be prayed with sincere meaning: "Bless this food to our use, and us to Thy service, and make us ever mindful of the needs of others. Amen."

Should you all fold your hands and bow your heads, or do you prefer to hold each other's hands in a circle? Of course, it doesn't really matter, because no one style is superior to any other. Whatever style of prayer you choose can become a calming source of security and identity for your children.

Some families extend their time of thanksgiving for the meal they are about to eat. They go around the table praying, taking turns saying simple prayers of blessing ("Bless Mom for cooking this good food.") or petition ("Lord, we're praying that You will help Dad find a new job."). A few families adopt the custom of praying both before and after the meal, *returning thanks* again after they have eaten.

Grace does not have to be a routine practiced only in the privacy of your own home. The apostle Paul prayed a grace before his last meal before he was shipwrecked. We read: "And when he had thus spoken, he took bread, and gave thanks to God in presence of them all: and when he had broken it, he began to eat" (Acts 27:35, KJV). And remember the time that Jesus prayed a special grace before He fed more than five thousand people: "Taking the five loaves and the two fish and looking up to heaven, he gave thanks and broke the loaves. Then he gave them to his disciples to set before the people" (Mark 6:41, NIV). You know what happened next!

In time, perhaps your family will have "grace stories" to share. "Remember the time we were saying grace when the tornado sirens went off?" Who can say whether or not those prayers that day saved your home from destruction?

You or your children may not feel comfortable about praying in public, but for some families, saying a brief grace when they are in a restaurant together is an unobtrusive way of witnessing to their family faith.

BEDTIME PRAYERS

Every night can include a special time of prayer with each of your children. Bedtime prayers can be much more than, "Now I lay me down to sleep…" and "Bless Grandma and Aunt Dolores." Each family will develop its own little rituals, and they will change as the children grow. Even older children who no longer need to be tucked in will appreciate a tradition of parental prayer at bedtime. It is a wonderful, built-in time for a child to be reminded of your unconditional love, which comes from and is blended with the love of their heavenly Father.

Bedtime is a natural time to reflect about the affairs of the day and to relinquish to God anything that remains unresolved. The Holy Spirit will help you *customize* your prayers together. Sometimes you may need to repent before your child for responding to him or her earlier in the day in an angry or unwarranted way. Following your lead, sometimes, also, your child may need to repent to you for disobedience or some other misdeed. "For we are all members of one body. 'In your anger do not sin': Do not let the sun go down while you are still angry, and do not give the devil a foothold" (Eph. 4:25–27, NIV).

At bedtime you can bring each child before the Father individually and lovingly. He created each one of your children with unique character traits that reveal part of His nature, and your prayers will take their differences into account. Part of being a good parent is developing your ability to recognize and affirm the positive traits of your children, rather than simply correcting them because you find them annoying. As you watch your children grow, let your prayers for each child be guided by your ongoing observations about their personalities and gifts. Ask the Holy Spirit to enhance and mold his or her traits as your son or daughter matures.

Teach your volatile son how to release his resentment about something that may have happened to him that day. Help your fearful daughter learn how to relax and trust God. Ask the Spirit to convert one child's stubbornness into a healthy kind of persistence and another child's tearful sensitivity into great compassion for other people.

Together, you and your child can pray for other family members and for anybody or anything that is of concern to your child. From time to time, be sure to remind each other that God has answered some of your earlier prayers, because surely He will do so.

"ANYTIME" PRAYERS

If you and your spouse communicate with God during the course of an average day as naturally as you do with each other, your children will learn to do the same. Let them "catch you" praying as you go about your daily agenda. Show them that prayer is not merely a hidden, private activity for grownups.

For instance, as you walk out the door together, you can speak out your trust that the Lord will guard and guide you. As you buckle your seatbelts in the car, you can pray for God's protection on the road. When one of your children falls down and comes to you crying, you can pray a comforting prayer as you patch up the damage. When one of them has a bad dream in the middle of the night, you can do the same. Before you send them off to school each morning, bless them with a brief prayer. At home or in public, without becoming insistent or embarrassing to your children, you can be reminding yourself that God is in charge, even as you apply to Him for the help you need.

LET YOUR CHILDREN PRAY FOR YOU

Turn the tables sometimes—ask your children, even your little ones, to pray for you. Without exceeding their maturity level to handle your difficulties, share some of your needs with them. Be real about it, not *religious*. After all, we have a *relationship* with our Father God. Just as we speak to our family members throughout the day, so we speak to God.

You can say, "I'm sad, honey. Would you pray for me, please?" "I'm a little scared about this. Please say a prayer that God will help me not to be afraid." Often, the childlike faith of your child will accomplish more in a one-sentence prayer than you can achieve with your anxious adult awareness.

Now, sometimes it can get humorous to ask your children to pray for you. I know a mother who, as she came up from bending to the floor to pick up a piece of dropped food, banged her head on the sharp underside of her son's high chair tray. It hurt so much that tears came to her eyes. As she held her head, kneeling in front of the high chair in front of her wide-eyed two-year-old, she moaned, "Oooh, Jimmy, please pray for Mommy!" So he put his little food-smeared hand on her face and prayed the only prayer he knew: "Dear Lord, fank You for dis good food!"

GOOD EXAMPLES

So much of the Spirit-empowered life is *caught*, not taught, and praying "without ceasing" (1 Thess. 5:17) is no exception.

I received a letter from a young mother from New Hampshire who described herself as "just an everyday, insignificant lady." When she began working with Concerned Women for America (CWA), she started attending regular meetings of her prayer chapter, bringing her three little girls—ages six, four, and two—along. She also took them when she went to pray outside abortion clinics.

One day she caught sight of her girls playing over in a corner of their family room. The six-year-old was holding a pretend CWA meeting for her sisters. They were praying for America. The child had seen her mother hand out flyers, so she had made some flyers of her own, one of which her mother sent to me. On the outside, it said: "CWA—We love children." Inside there were stick-figure children. "Mothers take care of their children," it said. On the back was printed: "We pray for one another."

"I never realized it," the mom wrote, "but while I was trying to make a change in my neighborhood, I was also influencing the lives of my own children."

Let your children know that you have a personal prayer time each day, even if you pray when they are asleep. As they grow up, encourage each one of them to have a short time alone with God every day, and make sure they have Bibles of their own. Show them that a habit of regular prayer is as life-giving as nourishing meals. All of us, young and old, are more eager to pray if we don't view it as a legalistic requirement.

Does God Answer?

Many people believe that all the promises in God's Word concerning prayer are made to everyone, and that anyone can claim them. Not so. These promises are made to God's children who keep His commandments, who do the things that are pleasing in His sight. As we have discussed already, not one of us is capable of being obedient to His commandments without the power of the Holy Spirit.

Proverbs 15:8 tells us that "the prayer of the upright is his [God's] delight" (KJV). And we read James 5:16: "The effective, fervent prayer of a righteous man avails much." Your righteousness is not your inherent goodness, nor is it earned by good behavior. A righteous person is one who has been *given* a right relationship with God by accepting

Christ as Savior. Only if you know God personally can you expect God to hear and answer your prayers.

This isn't to say that you are doing something terribly wrong if your prayers seem to go unanswered. Prayer, like any communication, doesn't always provide instant gratification or quick fixes. Recognizing this is just as much a part of being a Spirit-filled Christian as believing that God does answer prayer. Jesus said, "The wind blows wherever it pleases. You hear its sound, but you cannot tell where it comes from or where it is going. So it is with everyone born of the Spirit" (John 3:8, NIV).

JUANITA

Sometimes we are privileged to become part of God's answer to someone else's prayer. During a time of great upheaval in Nicaragua, I went with a group of people to nearby Costa Rica to distribute food and clothing to Nicaraguan refugees. Again and again, we heard the cry that families were cold at night and had no way to obtain blankets for warmth. We saw so many needs that it was hard to select the right ones to meet. But I just couldn't get the picture of those shivering little children out of my mind after I came home, especially when I saw my own grandchildren wrapped snugly in their own warm blankets at night.

I decided that God wanted me to make an appeal. So over the next few weeks, wherever I spoke I shared the cry of the refugees for blankets for their children. People started giving me money, and I took it with me on my next trip to Costa Rica. I gave it to the director of the refugee program, and he bought as many blankets as he could. He piled them in the back of his truck before we went to the camps on the northern border of Costa Rica.

We stopped at a little grass hut where an eighty-two-year-old woman named Juanita lived with her family. Juanita had walked through the jungle and over the mountains for three months just to escape the attacks of the Sandinistas and to get out of Nicaragua. She had arrived with only what she could carry on her back. The cataracts on her eyes were so bad she could hardly see, and her body ached with arthritis. Her bed was a wooden pallet in the corner of the shack she shared with nine other family members. The jungle nights were so cold that they shivered with no blankets. So she had started praying for one.

Her daughter didn't have Juanita's faith. "Nobody cares about us!" she told her mother. "We haven't got anything. We're way out here in the middle of the jungle. You're not going to get a blanket out here, so you might as well stop praying for it."

And then we walked into her hut. I saw Juanita's little frail body sitting on a wooden stool, and I walked over and wrapped a blanket around her. She looked at me as though I had just dropped out of heaven. Then she turned to her daughter and said matter-of-factly, "See? God heard my prayer. I knew He would bring me a blanket." Does God answer prayer? Ask Juanita.

SAMUEL'S BIBLE

A young architect in our church shared the most beautiful story I have ever heard about answered prayer. When he was a teenager, his youngest brother, Sam, lost his Bible in the Northwest woods while on a vacation with his parents. Another Christian family rented the cabin some time later and found the Bible, but no name or address inside. They did find this inscription on the first page: "To our son with love, Mom and Dad." By reading the notes this young man had carefully written throughout his Bible, the couple was so impressed with him that they called it to the attention of their children. That night at family devotions, the father prayed for this lad and then for his own teenage daughter, that someday the Lord would bring into her life a godly young man like the one who had owned the Bible.

Years passed, and they all forgot the experience. Eventually their daughter grew up and fell in love with a fine young man she met at a college-age youth camp, and they became engaged. One month before their wedding, the girl's parents were moving, and her fiancé came over to help them. As he picked up a box of books in the study, he saw an old Bible on the top. Setting the box down quickly, he examined it and exclaimed, "Where did you find my Bible?" Everyone was incredulous! Pointing to the inscription inside, he said, "See, it was given to me by my parents." Then, turning to the cover, he showed them the faded gold letters of his name, "Samuel," but his last name had been worn off. It seems that these two Christian families, who lived over a hundred miles apart and did not know each other, had rented the same cabin that summer, one week apart.

A Widow's Prayer

Tim and I have no trouble believing that story, and neither did my mother, Nellie Ratcliffe. The Ratcliffe family attended the First Baptist Church of Farmington, Michigan, shortly after a young widow who was a member of the church had moved to Detroit to live with relatives. My mother remembered the churchwomen praying for "Margaret," the young widow. Because my father had died when I was two years old, my mother felt moved to pray for this unknown woman that God would supernaturally supply her many needs and enable her to raise her children to serve the Lord. Years passed; Tim and I met in college and were married. One day we were discussing our family backgrounds, and Tim happened to mention that his family members had received Jesus Christ in the First Baptist Church of Farmington before his father died. Then we discovered that my family had moved there two months after his family had moved to Detroit. Would you believe that his widowed mother's first name was *Margaret*?

Yes, God does answer prayer, often in such wonderful ways that it's worth a long wait to find out about it!

Family Devotions

Last, but certainly not least, let's talk about *family devotions*. To some people, the term arouses negative feelings, but family worship time doesn't have to be a hardship. Even if your family spends only ten minutes a day at it, it's a worthwhile investment in the spiritual lives of each family member. Most families find fifteen minutes to be about right.

A family devotional time not only trains your children to acknowledge and respect God, but it also creates in them an early responsiveness to His Word as a book above all others, one that should be read daily. Your chosen time can be first thing in the morning or in the early evening, after the evening meal. Establish your devotional time as a priority whenever you decide to have it, even if it's once a week on Sunday night or on Mondays, Wednesdays, and Fridays after the dishes are done and it's too dark to play outside any longer.

As parents, you need to set the agenda, the tone, and the pace. "Wing and a prayer" devotions will falter in no time. Daily devotions provide an opportunity for parents to teach their children to pray and to discuss principles from the Bible, but you don't need to become a Bible scholar to do so. Your Bible bookstore can supply you with good age-appropriate books to use. Your family preferences will provide you with ideas.

Here is a rough outline of a family devotional time:

1. Read the Bible aloud—one chapter or less, depending on the ages of your children. If they are young, keep the reading to a Bible story that can be discussed later. Older children can read Scripture passages that teach them how to live the Christian life.

2. Or you may choose to read something from a daily devotional guide.

3. Then briefly discuss what you have read. Ask your children simple questions.

4. Review a Scripture memory verse together.

5. Pray aloud together. Depending on your family size, you may not have time for everyone to speak.

6. Sing a song of praise to God. Keep it simple and meaningful.

This is just a rough outline. Your family requirements and preferences may cause you to make creative adaptations. For instance, if "the natives are restless" some busy day, you could declare a Parade Day. Give each child instruments (even car keys to jingle and plastic bowls to beat on), and march around your house singing lively Bible songs from their vacation Bible school. Or if one of your teenagers is studying a foreign language in school, ask him to come prepared to say a prayer in that language. Ask your earnest preteen to give a personal application of the Bible lesson of the day. Some devotional guides are especially inventive, leading listeners through adventure stories or posing stimulating questions.

Even if you are a professional preacher or teacher, please don't make your family devotions into a time for preaching at your family. Your children will get much more out of family devotions if they feel they are contributing members of your time together.

"OUR FATHER..."

If you haven't already done so at bedtime, you could use your family devotional time to teach your children the Lord's Prayer. Show them where it appears in the Bible. (Jesus taught it to His disciples, and you can read about it in Matthew 6:9–13 and Luke 11:2–4.)

The Lord's Prayer is the perfect model prayer. You could expand upon one line at a time to show your family how well it covers all the aspects of prayer:

> ✦ *"Our Father in heaven, hallowed be Your name"*—recognizes that God is a loving and perfect Father who is worthy of our praise.

Our praise consists of both *adoration* (honoring God for who He is) and *thanksgiving* (honoring Him for what He has done).

* *"Your kingdom come. Your will be done on earth as it is in heaven"*—provides us with words of agreement with God's will as it applies to our little corner of the earth as well as the affairs of the whole world.

* *"Give us this day our daily bread"*—shows us that yes, it's all right to ask for anything we need, not merely for our literal bread.

* *"Forgive us our debts [sins, trespasses]"*—reminds us to keep our hearts cleansed by asking the Lord for forgiveness for our sins.

* *"As we forgive our debtors [those who sin against us]"*—encourages us to forgive others, repeatedly if necessary.

* *"Deliver us from the evil one"*—makes sure that we ask for protection from harm as well as courage to resist temptation.

* *"For Yours is the kingdom and the power and the glory forever. Amen"*—acknowledges that He is the highest, the strongest, the best, and the most wonderful Lord of all!

PRAYER LOG

Your family devotional time or your family mealtime is an ideal opportunity to review a family *prayer log*. Record specific prayer requests in one column, with dates—and the answers, also with dates—in the adjacent column. Any child who is old enough to write can contribute to the prayer log. Sometimes you will find that your prayers have been answered in less than twenty-four hours. Other times, rereading the prayer log will stimulate you to continued perseverance in prayer. It's always an enriching experience to review the earlier pages of the prayer log to see how many prayers (especially the ones everybody forgot about) were answered.

✦ ✦ ✦ ✦ ✦

Your home is the crucible of your Christian life, where ordinary family tensions provide an ongoing testing ground for your faith. No member of the family can make a success of it without the help of the Holy Spirit. And family prayer—both regular and spontaneous—is the only way of guaranteeing that the Holy Spirit will be invited into your family often enough to make a difference.

SPIRITUAL POWER FOR YOUR FAMILY: PRAYER

Our Father in heaven,

Thank You for sending us a Savior and for providing us with Your Holy Spirit. Thank You for making it possible for me and for my family to live with You in eternal joy.

Thank You also for making it possible for us to come before You anytime, anyplace, in prayer. Please forgive me for not following You every time You have said, "Come to Me." Now I want to follow You wholeheartedly, and I want my family to come, too.

I trust You to provide the resources we will need to "bloom where we are planted" in this family and to become rooted and grounded in Your Word. We need more of Your love. We need to hear from You. I ask You to plant in each of us an unshakable desire to follow after You.

It is so good to belong to you. Amen.

Part Two

Yielding
to the
Spirit's Design

CHAPTER 5

Becoming a Spirit-Empowered Wife

J ESUS TELLS US that the happiness we seek depends upon *hearing* the Word of God and *obeying* it:

> Blessed [happy] rather are those who hear the word of God
> and obey it.
> —LUKE 11:28, NIV

As we have been discovering in this book, the only possible way that we can manage to obey God's Word is by the power of the Holy Spirit.

What does it mean—specifically for a wife—to hear and to obey God's Word? I want to consider wives first, not only because I am a wife myself, but also because in the Bible's longest text on family life, Ephesians 5:22–6:4, Paul speaks first to wives. I believe he addresses wives first for a good reason: in a family, she is the link between the husband and the children, and she will tend to draw the rest of her family along whatever path she takes.

A Spirit-controlled wife makes a Spirit-filled home possible.

The "S" Word

So what does God's Word have to say to wives?

> Wives, submit to your own husbands, as to the Lord. For the husband is head of the wife, as also Christ is head of the church; and He is the Savior of the body. Therefore, just as the church is subject to Christ, so let the wives be to their own husbands in everything.
> —Ephesians 5:22–24

There it is. It's unavoidable. The "S" word—*submit*. Apparently, to be obedient to the Word, a wife needs to submit to her husband. Many capable and intelligent women reject the very thought of being subject to their husbands. No healthy woman wants to be a *doormat*. To them, it seems that God must have a grudge against women. Most of them would prefer equality between the sexes, a 50/50 arrangement.

But is that what it means to be subject to a husband and submissive to Christ Jesus? Objectors cite Paul's statement in Galatians 3:28, in which he writes, "There is neither Jew nor Greek, there is neither slave nor free, there is neither male nor female; for you are all one in Christ Jesus." They expand this single line into a principle of across-the-board social equality between men and women. It is true that men and women are on equal footing in their individual relationships with God and in their access to His Holy Spirit. Yet, within marriage, the position of women and men has been established by the order of their creation—Adam first, then Eve. After the Fall, the subordination of the wife became greater than it had been, as God said to Eve:

74

I will greatly increase your pains in childbearing; with pain you will give birth to children. Your desire will be for your husband, and he will rule over you.

—Genesis 3:16, niv

Upon the man, God laid the authority to rule and rule well, which is a difficult role, one that Adam already had failed to do. Many men gladly abdicate their responsibilities.

God told Adam and Eve that this arrangement was a burden brought on by their disobedience. Throughout human history, men and women have felt this burden, and yet its very oppressiveness reveals the way the burden can become a blessing: *through God's help alone can both the woman and the man achieve the balance that will bring blessing.*

God's order is *better* than 50/50—He wants an arrangement in which the wife, enabled by the Holy Spirit, is 100 percent a godly, happy woman, and the husband, also enabled by the Spirit, is 100 percent a godly, happy man. He has sent us His Holy Spirit to empower us to do what would otherwise be impossible.

Do not be deceived by outspoken critics of God's order for wives. It is impossible to follow their program and remain Spirit-controlled women. Claiming to speak for all women, they are rebels against Him, preferring their own ways to His. As loudly as they proclaim "freedom," they will never experience true liberty until they meet Jesus Christ. He's the one who, when He walked the earth, honored women more than the rest of the culture did. He still does so today.

Helpmeet

The critics always complain that submissiveness is the same as servility. But a wife who meekly says, "Whatever you decide, dear," when an unwise husband is steering the family toward destruction is not being properly submissive—she is abdicating her role.

God has appointed her as a "helpmeet" for her husband. She should not be passive. Under the protection of her husband, she actively contributes her intelligent opinions and her wisdom to her husband, who needs her to do so.

> And the LORD God said, It is not good that man should be alone; I will make him an help meet for him.
> —GENESIS 2:18, KJV

From "an help meet," which means "a helper suitable," comes our English word *helpmeet* or *helpmate*.

A helpmeet can adequately fulfill the needs of her partner. She is not inferior to him; she serves with him with all her capabilities, choosing to situate herself as his right-hand helper.

She is free to choose, by the way. And because she has decided to follow God's ordained pattern, not to cling to her *rights*, but to submit her free will to her husband, she is accorded many privileges and blessings that would otherwise elude her.

God has given great gifts to women, and they are greatly enhanced in a Spirit-filled woman. Women are as intelligent as men, and their stamina and stability are often as great as or greater than that of men. Women possess leadership gifts, and God honors them for using those gifts. Consider some of the women of the Bible: Miriam, who defied Pharaoh and saved Moses' life; Deborah, who served as a prophetess and judge in Israel; Esther, the queen who risked death to save her people; Priscilla, who, with her husband, Aquila, was a tentmaker and leader in the early church; and—most "blessed among women"—Mary, the mother of Jesus, who is honored above all the others for submitting both to the Holy Spirit and to her earthly husband, Joseph.

A submissive helpmeet is not silenced or suppressed. She offers her insights and shares her feelings with her husband, even when she doesn't agree with him. Submission doesn't close her mouth, shut off her brain, or make her surrender her individuality.

TRUE SUBMISSION

A Spirit-filled helpmeet does not subject herself to her husband only when he is nice to her or after he has proven to be trustworthy. No, she submits to him because she wants to be obedient to God. She doesn't want any separation between herself and God's Spirit. The degree of her submission is a measure or a barometer of her relationship to Jesus. She has been charged to submit to her husband "as to the Lord" (Eph. 5:22). Verses 23–24 compare her relationship with her husband to the church's relationship with Christ Jesus. Just as every Christian surrenders to Jesus, a wife lays down her self-will and leaves the results up to God.

True submission is in force when the wife's attitudes and actions have come into complete agreement with her husband's. She can't pretend to be submissive while carrying objections in her heart.

Tim and I have found in our own marriage that we commonly see things differently. But he listens to my opinion with respect and considers it carefully before proceeding. From time to time, I have unduly influenced him in a decision that we regretted. This has caused me to ponder my remarks more carefully, making sure they represent true wisdom, for they carry so much weight with him.

Once I was leading a woman's Bible study on this passage from Ephesians. A troubled wife interrupted me, "Why is it that the woman gets the most difficult part of the marriage relationship, that of submitting?"

Before I could answer, a transformed rebel replied, "I must disagree with you. The husband has the most difficult position. He is responsible for making final decisions that affect the future of his wife and children. All I am required to do is submit to him and serve as his helpmeet. The blame or glory for decisions falls solely on him." That stimulated a very lively discussion. We concluded that God's assignments to husbands and wives were not made according to their individual abilities, but rather to their utter dependence upon the One who enables them to fulfill their assigned roles and who will grant to each of them unusual wisdom.

In God's eyes, their roles are balanced: "Nevertheless, neither is man independent of woman, nor woman independent of man, in the Lord" (1 Cor. 11:11). The man is the head of the woman, but women give birth to men. The wife submits to her husband as to the Lord, because he sits in the place of Christ in authority and responsibility. As the head of the family, he is the image and glory of God, whereas she is "the glory of man" (v. 7). Neither assignment is easy, but each role can be fulfilled when the Holy Spirit is in control of their lives.

Wives are to be helpmeets to their own husbands, not to all men in general. Some extreme teachings have grown from this biblical injunction, including the false idea that single girls should be under the authority of their single male dates. Do not misconstrue the explicit limits of this scriptural command. The wife is to respect and reverence her own husband. However, while she is still single, she should be asking herself whether a prospective husband is one to whom she could lovingly submit after marriage. If not, she shouldn't marry him, because their marriage will be at risk of failing.

A wife is attracted to the qualities in her husband that distinguish him from other men. She is attracted to his manly leadership of the home. If she refuses to submit to him and begins to dominate him, she will destroy the very part of him that God designed for her benefit, his leadership capability.

After more than fifty years of marriage, twenty-five years of which I have been leading a ministry that is independent of my husband's, I can testify that being his helpmeet is the most fulfilling part of my life. He is my very best friend, and he still makes my heart beat faster every time I see him. I love being 100 percent submitted to him.

UNEQUALLY YOKED?

What if your husband is not a Spirit-filled Christian? Large numbers of Christian women are married to husbands who have not accepted Jesus Christ as Savior and Lord. Even here, submission is commanded:

> Wives, likewise, be submissive to your own husbands, that
> even if some do not obey the word, they, without a word,
> may be won by the conduct of their wives.
>
> —1 PETER 3:1

This verse refers back to the preceding verses, in which Jesus' example has been put forward. An "unequally yoked" wife has clear instructions: with the help of the Holy Spirit, become as much like your Lord as you can, and your Christlike behavior in your home will win your husband to Jesus. No amount of nagging or preaching can achieve that result; in fact, that may well drive your husband away from God. Apologize to your husband for your fleshly actions and reactions, and tell him that you are going to be trying to "practice what you preach" from now on. It will be humbling, but you will carry through to victory. The appeal of the gospel message is undeniable in a changed life of a loving wife.

Submission remains the key word, with the only exception being if the husband asks his wife to do something that is contrary to the Bible's teachings, such as stealing or committing adultery. In those cases, "We ought to obey God rather than men" (Acts 5:29).

A SPIRIT-FILLED TEMPERAMENT

Even if you have been married a long time, as I have, your experience is not going to be the same as mine. Christian wives have not been reproduced from the same cookie cutter. We come from different backgrounds, we look different, and we possess diverse temperaments.

For the first fifteen years of my marriage, I didn't like being different from other wives who seemed to be better looking or at least more talented. Always trying to measure up to someone else's expectations, including Tim's, made me fearful and introverted.

Even after I learned about the Holy Spirit and became filled with His power to be free from my feelings of inadequacy, I found it hard to imagine what "free" would look like. Step by step, I had to follow His leading to become fully the woman He had created me to be.

One of the biggest breakthroughs came when I began to understand that my God-given temperament—the set of identifiable traits with which I was born—would be where most of the Spirit's work in me would occur. As I permitted Him to do so, He worked His holiness into my temperament, bringing each trait under the master plan of His lordship. I'm still a work in progress, and I'm happy to report that I'm happier with the results!

Here are the basics of what I discovered. I learned that people possess unique combinations of traits and that those traits, combined with our upbringing, our reactions to life experiences, and our education, will determine how we behave. The traits fall into four broad categories. (I have written in much more detail about this subject in my book *The Spirit-Controlled Woman*.)

- Introverts—
    Melancholic
    Phlegmatic

- Extroverts—
    Choleric
    Sanguine

Melancholic

A woman who is predominantly melancholic will have a sensitive nature. She will be a deep thinker who is emotionally responsive to her environment and to others. A conscientious worker, she can be very gifted and creative. She will be a faithful friend, although she makes friends cautiously, and she can be critical of their imperfections. The downside of her makeup is that she can be moody and even gloomy. Others may find her hard to get along with. It's hard for her to forgive. She may tend to be a hypochondriac or introspective to an unhealthy degree.

As she yields to the work of the Spirit in her life, she will find that her greatest challenges involve overcoming her critical and self-absorbed tendencies in favor of developing a thankful heart. As a wife, she may be sabotaging her marriage by harboring negative thoughts about her husband. With God's help, she can come to appreciate his good qualities, and her natural loyalty will make her a stalwart and exceptional helpmeet to him.

Phlegmatic

A phlegmatic woman is cheerful and easy to get along with, a good listener, and a faithful friend. She gives advice only when asked, but this can be partly because she lacks confidence in herself. She can be a worrier, and she can be stingy, although by and large she is kind and calm. Others may interpret her passivity and introversion as an attitude of superiority. She covers awkwardness with a witty sense of humor and keeps herself somewhat removed from the people around her.

As a wife, her easygoing nature makes her pleasant to live with. She is not a natural leader, so she will not challenge her husband in the driver's seat of their marriage. Although her seeming indifference and her reluctance to make changes can bother a husband who has a different personality from hers, she will provide a stable home for their children and teach them a practical, easy way of approaching life.

Choleric

A choleric woman is a natural leader; she was born to be in charge. She is goal-oriented and impatient with aesthetic considerations; she would rather organize a fund-raising concert than listen to the music. She is doggedly determined, and she is often considered to be more intelligent than she really is. Fearlessness and optimism are part of her makeup, but so are insensitivity and anger. While she may believe in the Spirit-filled life and may even understand her own temperament to some degree, she will tend to think that this information is for other people and not for her.

There can be only one head of the family, and that head should be the husband. A choleric wife may find this hard to accept. At times, the fur may fly! On the other hand, she is decisive, she has energy to spare, and she responds to emergencies quickly. If she can cooperate with the Spirit's direction, she will be able to learn to be more sensitive to and cooperative with others.

Sanguine

A sanguine woman is not a deep thinker, but everybody likes her. She makes them feel good even when she's having a hard time herself. She may have a weight problem, because her forte is not willpower, and her emotions are always on the surface. This is also revealed in her failure to plan ahead, which will create a series of crises in her life. At least she apologizes easily and never bears a grudge. She is almost always friendly and smiling.

With the help of the Holy Spirit, a sanguine wife's flightiness can be tamed, and her natural charm will be enhanced. She can learn both to smell the roses and follow through on her obligations, although she will have to work at it.

Combinations

Almost nobody falls into one single category; most of us combine an interesting variety of traits. For example, my husband, who knows me best, says that I am a mixture of three of the temperaments. My primary one is phlegmatic, but my secondary temperament involves both the choleric and the sanguine. With God's grace and patience with me, I believe He is helping me to overcome some of the shortcomings of these temperaments. However, He is not finished with me yet.

Even strong-willed choleric women can become submissive wives. I know one such lady who had all but destroyed her marriage with her rapier wit and forceful personality, running the entire family single-handedly. She happened to be a very able Bible teacher. One day the

Holy Spirit brought her under conviction while she was preparing a lesson based on the verses in Ephesians 5 about the Christian family. She was shocked to realize that the real cause of the friction in her marriage was because she was always snatching the leadership role away from her husband. It meant that she was not really the spiritual woman she claimed to be. She repented deeply and made herself accountable to the Holy Spirit and her husband until she became fully submissive to him. Today they enjoy a happy, model marriage.

Like choleric women, sanguine wives may find it more difficult to surrender the reins to their husbands. Women who possess phlegmatic or melancholy temperaments, however, will find it relatively easy to let their husbands lead.

If you want to investigate your own temperament further, look for helpful resources such as *The Spirit-Controlled Woman*. The point to remember is that no woman is naturally equipped to be the perfect wife, because only a Spirit-filled and Spirit-empowered wife has the necessary resources to obey the Word of God. We glorify God as we allow Him to redeem every part of our human nature.

THE WIFE AS HOME MANAGER

The husband is to be the supervisor of the home, but the wife will do the actual managing. This does not mean that she will make all the decisions or do all the work, but she will tend to be more involved in the day-to-day operation of the household. She will make decisions based on the general policies that she and her husband have formulated together.

In his book *The Christian Home*, Norman V. Williams refers to the origins of the words *husband* and *wife*. The word *husband* used to be *house-band,* in other words, the one who "bands" or "binds" the home together with strength, provision, and stability. In contrast, the word *wife* comes from *weaver*—in other words, the one who uses her clever hands to weave the beautiful fabric of family life.

Too often, women say, "I'm just a homemaker," as if they may have missed a higher calling. Perhaps it will help them to respect their role more highly if they think of themselves as home managers. The challenges of their job are so numerous that the position rivals any professional management-level career.

This has been true at least since before the time of the "super-woman" in Proverbs 31—about whom I used to refrain from reading because she intimidated me. (I considered her standards far beyond my reach.) Now, from the vantage point of maturity and after having experienced firsthand the abundant help of the Holy Spirit, I reformulated a few of the verses for the modern, Spirit-empowered wife:

    Proverbs 31:10. An excellent wife is hard to find. She cannot be bought with expensive jewels or fancy sports cars. Her inner beauty exceeds what mere money can buy.

    31:11. Her husband trusts her with all of his possessions. He is not concerned that she will drain their bank account or run up the charge account. He is confident that she will help them establish financial security.

    31:12. She is a devoted helpmeet, responding to his love and living for his fulfillment.

    31:13. She decorates their home in a way that suits their income and lifestyle, and she keeps it tidy, even mopping the kitchen floor with a song in her heart and praise on her lips.

    31:14. She shops wisely for food and provides well-balanced, nutritious meals for her family.

    31:15. She rises early to make sure that her husband and family are cared for.

    31:16. She earns extra money to help with the family expenses.

❧ *31:17.* She takes good care of her body, exercising regularly to keep fit and strong.

❧ *31:18.* She balances her busy life so she can keep going far well into the evening.

❧ *31:19.* She keeps her mind and hands busy even when she is sitting down.

❧ *31:20.* She makes time to assist those who are needy, providing food and service.

❧ *31:21.* She is a season ahead, making sure she has warm winter clothes for her children even before the snow begins to fall.

❧ *31:22.* She selects her own modest wardrobe carefully and stays well groomed, not dressing to get attention.

❧ *31:23.* Her husband is respected among the leaders of the community and in the neighborhood.

❧ *31:24.* She attends a prayer group to pray for needs beyond those of her family.

❧ *31:25.* Charm and self-confidence are her characteristics, and she faces the future with joy and hope.

❧ *31:26.* She speaks with wisdom that comes from studying the Word of God, and her life is an example of kindness to others.

❧ *31:27.* She manages her home with great care and does not sit idly watching TV or chatting with her friends on the telephone.

❧ *31:28.* Her children love and respect her, and her husband sings her praises, saying:

≪ 31:29. "You, my darling, are the greatest woman God could have given me."

≪ 31:30. Charm and a beautiful face can be deceiving, but a woman who reveres the Lord shall be praised.

≪ 31:31. Her children and her community, who know her well, will see all that she has done and will admire and praise her.

Did you catch the theme that runs through every activity of the Proverbs 31 woman? Everything she does is centered around her home and family. She is the "weaver" who intertwines the different threads of the home to produce the finished product. Some of her hard-earned, on-the-job qualities are as follows:

≪ Inner beauty, developed from walking in the Spirit
≪ Trustworthiness, faithfulness
≪ Prudence
≪ Submissiveness
≪ Tenderness
≪ Cheerfulness
≪ Carefulness, tidiness
≪ Resourcefulness, capability
≪ Alertness
≪ Creativity
≪ Willingness
≪ Astuteness
≪ Compassion
≪ Dedication to the Word and her family
≪ High principles, modesty

The Christian wife certainly does not need to feel inferior or oppressed. In fact, sometimes her job may seem to be bigger than she can handle, which brings us back to the main theme of this chapter: we cannot grow into our role as Christian wives without outside help from God's Spirit.

The Spirit-filled home manager will say in her heart:

> Whatever [I] do, [I] work at it with all [my] heart, as working for the Lord, not for men, since [I] know that [I] will receive an inheritance from the Lord as a reward. It is the Lord Christ [I am] serving.
>
> —Colossians 3:23–24, NIV

Spiritual Power for Your Family: Prayer

Dear Lord,

It's a tall order to be a Christian wife and mother, and I thank You from the bottom of my heart for giving me Your Holy Spirit to help me along the way.

Keep me alert to Your conviction and correction, and let me have the encouragement of seeing positive changes in myself. I want to be a blessing to my husband and children. With Your help, I can pass on to my children the firsthand knowledge of what a Spirit-empowered wife and mother looks like.

I am grateful and humble. In Your service and in Your name, amen.

Chapter 6

Wife as Lover, Wife as Mother

THE BIBLE SAYS more to husbands about loving their wives than it does to wives about loving their husbands. Maybe that's because wives don't need as much advice. By nature, women seem to find it easier to love. They seem to be willing to make a greater effort to be good and faithful lovers, and, conversely, they are also more willing to settle for a second-rate love life.

Love is not a one-sided affair. It develops out of mutual esteem and admiration. If love is not nurtured, it can be warped, and it can be destroyed. Even as the natural nurturer, every wife needs to be sure she remains the best lover her husband could ever have.

"TEMPERAMENTAL" LOVER

There is nothing more significant to our ability to love than the temperaments with which we were born. Our mix of temperament traits produces our actions and reactions.

I am convinced that the best lovers are married Christians who are filled with the Spirit and who have allowed Him to *temper* their temperaments. One reason I feel so strongly about this is because of a survey Tim and I administered to seven hundred couples before we wrote our book *The Act of Marriage*. The results showed Christians scoring ten points higher in sexual satisfaction than non-Christian couples. Moreover, Spirit-filled Christians rated their satisfaction seven points higher than the non-Spirit-controlled Christians.

With your given temperament, how can you become the best wife you can possibly be? Here are some thoughts:

If you are a *melancholy* wife, you will find that your love life is characterized by mood swings, which can be at turns good or bad, from supreme romantic ecstasy to outright rejection of your husband. You can be an exciting partner and enjoy great fulfillment if you learn to walk in the Spirit rather than in the mood of the moment. You may be afflicted with prudishness, which will make it more difficult for you to relax in your marriage. Asking the help of the Spirit, you will need to be careful to repair any damage you do when you allow some aspect of your husband's behavior to turn you against him. You will also need to be careful about self-pity. Ask God to give you an unconditional love for your husband—both of you will be rewarded.

If you are a *phlegmatic* wife, your naturally passive personality will make you as easy to get along with in the bedroom as you are in the car or in the kitchen, and you won't tend to withhold your affection. However, if you are disappointed with your husband's love, you may notice that you satisfy your need to give love by turning your attention to your friends or children. In general, your biggest problems will involve fears rather than relationship issues. One unusual problem of a phlegmatic wife is that she often already adequately exemplifies Christian virtues, so she may not realize she's a sinner in need of a Savior. Don't let self-righteousness or passivity keep you out of the kingdom of God. In addition, don't allow your passivity to dominate your appearance. Make the extra effort, asking for the help of God's Spirit, to keep yourself well groomed and to maintain a neat home.

If you are a *choleric* wife, you will already recognize that you can squash your husband's ego all too easily—and at the peril of losing the ability both of you need to love each other. You will need to learn how to rely on the Holy Spirit in order to achieve the sweetness of disposition that improves any marriage. Learn how to encourage your husband; it won't come naturally to you. Your potential in the bedroom will depend upon your growing-up experiences. Positive role models and experiences will ensure that you will succeed, but negative examples and incidents will make you shut down, and you may need help to overcome internal reservations. Learn how to forgive men who have hurt you; otherwise, you will be caught in a trap of anger and criticism. Are you a night person? Choleric people often are. If you want to stay up much later than your husband does, consider going to bed earlier so that you can be with him.

If you are a *sanguine* wife, your natural charm and friendliness will enhance your ability to be a good lover. You might want to watch out, however, that you don't (inadvertently) give the wrong signals to other men around you. Since sanguine wives rarely carry a grudge, your husband will hardly ever have to worry about getting the cold shoulder from you. You are affectionate and able to "turn on a dime" even when you don't feel in a loving mood. You are not a passive lover, which most likely he will enjoy. Your tremendous desire to please your husband may entail making changes in your grooming, manners, housekeeping, or whatever would please him. But you can pull it off—if he lovingly motivates you.

THINK POSITIVE

A woman's brain is "control central" where her love life is concerned. As she thinks, so she is. (See Proverbs 23:7.) She cannot rise above her expectations. When she anticipates failure, she will fail. However, when she anticipates success, she improves her possibilities greatly. It has very little to do with her IQ, not much to do with age and experience, and is equally applied to all temperament types. Her mental attitude alone will determine how good a lover she is.

Three areas of her thinking exercise the most influence:

1. *What she thinks about lovemaking.* God is the author of sex, and He made it enjoyable for both men and women. It is not merely something for a wife to endure "for the sake of the man's pleasure," but a marvelous fulfillment of their unity with each other.

2. *What she thinks about herself.* Self-criticism and self-rejection run rampant with women. If she learns to regard herself as appealing and responsive, she will have the capability of becoming even more so.

3. *What she thinks about her husband.* Faultfinding destroys love. Appreciation enhances it. Even a wife who already encourages her husband can benefit from reviewing his good qualities.

Your husband cannot read your mind. He will take his cues from your demeanor and your appearance. If you always meet him at the end of a long workday in a bedraggled condition, he will not get the message that he's special.

Besides keeping yourself as attractive as you can, another way to show him how special he is to you is to *go the extra mile* to serve him. It might not be very glamorous, but both of you will see the difference it makes. I'm thinking of an example from our early life together.

After only a few weeks of marriage, I had discovered that I would find Tim's socks each morning right where he had removed his shoes the night before. They were always rolled up in little round balls. At first I enjoyed picking up his socks for him, and it didn't hurt me to do it. But the days wore into weeks and the weeks into months. I started to become a little irritated when I picked them up. I began to wonder who had picked up after him before he met me. It occurred to me that maybe he didn't know we had a clothes hamper.

So I introduced him to this special piece of equipment. Nevertheless, I continued to stumble over the dirty socks each morning. Stumble? Yes, because they were growing in size—at least in my mind. "He's a healthy man," I grumbled. "He should pick up his own socks."

Those two socks irritated me so much that I became critical of other things my husband was doing. When he came home in the evening, I stopped seeing a wonderful husband who loved me. Instead, I saw only the wearer of those dirty socks!

One gloomy day, I picked up the Bible by the nightstand and read a verse, "And whatever you do in word or deed, do all in the name of the Lord Jesus, giving thanks to God the Father through Him" (Col. 3:17). To my mind, it seemed to be saying, "When you pick up your husband's dirty socks, do it in the name of the Lord Jesus, giving thanks to God and the Father by Him." Then I read on, "Wives, submit to your own husbands, as is fitting in the Lord" (v. 18). And verses 23–24: "And whatever you do, do it heartily, as to the Lord and not to men, knowing that from the Lord you will receive the reward of the inheritance; for you serve the Lord Christ."

I wasn't just picking up dirty socks; I was serving the Lord Jesus.

I confessed my rotten attitude to the Lord, and after that I truly did enjoy serving my husband and the Lord Jesus each day as I picked up those blessed, dirty socks.

The result? Somehow those socks began to disappear on their own. One day he just decided to be more careful, and he started picking them up himself. I must admit, I missed his blessed socks because they reminded me of this spiritual lesson.

CHECK YOUR INHIBITIONS

Modesty is an admirable virtue in a woman, but we must be careful not to define it too narrowly in the bedroom. We read that Adam and Eve were "naked, and they felt no shame" (Gen. 2:25, NIV). That means they were *un*inhibited.

If you feel that you have "hang-ups," don't be ashamed to ask for help. Perhaps you know a godly, happily married woman you can trust. Ask her to help you define "uninhibited," and ask the Holy Spirit to bring you into new freedom. There is no gold standard here, but there is a lot of pure joy to be mined.

Communicate freely with your husband. He needs to know your perceptions and feelings because, contrary to popular opinion, men do not emerge into adulthood knowing everything there is to know about sex. They may have been interested in the subject since kindergarten, but their sources of information are often faulty, especially if they have believed some of the braggadocio they have heard in the locker room.

A wife may have only one lover in her lifetime, only one man who will know her intimately. Her ability to overcome her hang-ups, share herself freely, and respond to her husband deeply will make their love life an exciting and rewarding experience. A relaxed wife is much more responsive sexually. Her calm smile reassures her husband and inspires him to love her more tenderly.

Remember that men are stimulated by sight as well as by their other senses. What do you wear to bed? You might want to reconsider your priorities if you're still sleeping in the same oversized T-shirt you've had since high school or you've decided that your complexion requires an overnight mud mask treatment.

Restoration

Years ago after presenting a Family Life Seminar, Tim was approached by an attractive twenty-six-year-old mother of three who said, "Would you explain why I am unable to respond to my husband after six years of marriage?" She described her husband as kind and considerate.

Tim was short on time, but the Holy Spirit inspired him to ask just the right question: "What was your relationship with your father like?"

Her face became distorted as she berated her father. "He is the biggest hypocrite I have ever seen. He is an official in this church, yet he molested both of my younger sisters and tried to molest me."

Tim responded, "I believe that your unforgiveness of your father is blocking your love for your husband. You had better forgive your father. You cannot indulge in bitterness toward him without having it spill over into your other relationships."

"But he doesn't deserve it!"

"No, but your husband does! You are not responsible for your father's behavior, but you are responsible for your reaction to it. God will help you to forgive him." Crying, she dropped to her knees and confessed her sin.

A year later at another seminar in the same city, she met Tim again, this time with her husband. "Thanks, preacher," he said, crushing Tim in a bear hug, "My wife's a different woman!"

Pray

The Holy Spirit will not blush if you pray about your love life. It's not as if you need to pray about it aloud at the midweek church prayer meeting. Just pray silently or perhaps together with your husband.

Ask God to help you whenever you feel that something is stalling your love life. Expect that He will direct you to an adequate solution. "Until now you have not asked for anything in my name. Ask and you will receive, and your joy will be complete" (John 16:24, NIV).

INNER—AND OUTER—BEAUTY

Should a woman's beauty make any difference? I'm talking not only of her physical, feminine appearance, but also of the "hidden woman of the heart."

This matters more than you might think, because a woman's appearance—her grooming, her size, her carriage—mirrors her character and, above all, indicates who controls her life, Jesus Christ or herself. Inner beauty can come only from walking with God, and outer beauty is a testimony to godliness, manifesting what is truly in a woman's heart.

This is a misunderstood concept, to be sure. Many Christians believe that paying attention to one's looks is tantamount to idolatry, or that the "natural look" is closer to God's ideal, or that we should simply cover each other's failings with unconditional love. Of course, there is a degree of truth in each of those viewpoints. But how does an out-of-shape, tired, and crabby woman reflect Jesus to the people around her? As excusers of self-indulgence, proponents of the "who cares?" school will find one day that they have declined into an unkempt, unhealthy, faded, wrinkled look that does not represent God's vibrant life.

On the opposite side are the women who own more beauty products than the local salon and whose weekly schedule is jammed with beauty-enhancing classes, treatments, and appointments. Their message? "I care more about what *I* look like than I care about anything else."

Pursuing either extreme betrays a lack of liberty and trust in God, and it contradicts the promise of Philippians 4:19: "And my God shall supply all your need according to His riches in glory by Christ Jesus." The overdone woman is trying too hard to supply her own need, compensating for her lack of security in Christ. The "underdone" woman is actually motivated by a similar lack of security. Our goal should be to be growing in our faith-filled liberty in the Spirit, which will inevitably result in increased lightness in our step and brightness in our eyes.

We need to start by taking God's unconditional love, which makes it possible to accept ourselves as we are, and then ask Him to help us change the things that can be changed. We have already talked about how God can improve our personal temperaments. Now we need to consider how our Spirit-controlled temperament will be mirrored in our physical appearance and carriage.

I am reminded of the biblical Esther, who was given one year for beautification to prepare for her marriage to the king. Becoming far more than merely a "knockout" princess, Esther's extraordinary obedience, courage, and wisdom have made her beautiful even to those who have known her only through the words on a printed page. I think also of the description of the Proverbs 31 woman; she wears beautiful clothes of purple and pure linen, and yet the writer devotes most of his words to praising her for her fine character. You see, inner and outer beauty walk hand in hand.

"Gentle and quiet spirit"

Standards of feminine beauty change with time and geography, but one standard rules them all for a Christian woman: her outward adorning should not be so extreme as to call attention to itself. Her inner beauty should shine through. Remember the passage that reads, "Your beauty should not come from outward adornment, such as braided hair and the wearing of gold jewelry and fine clothes. Instead, it should be that of your inner self, the unfading beauty of a gentle and quiet spirit, which is of great worth in God's sight" (1 Pet. 3:3–4, NIV). This is not saying that all outward adorning is wrong, but rather that it is sinful when it takes priority over the inner adornment of a trusting and peace-filled spirit.

In other words, putting on nice clothes, going to a hairdresser, or wearing jewelry are not inherently evil. What matters is the priority of these practices in our lives. We don't want other people to be distracted from matters of the heart by our showy outfit—or blinded to the testimony of our inner beauty by the run-down condition of our outer shell.

Let your outward appearance become a frame to surround a picture of the hidden person of your heart. A beautifully framed picture is one that does not draw attention to the frame, but one in which the frame aids the viewer to center his attention on the picture itself. Each of us can discover from God what our "frame" should look like.

I define a "gentle and quiet spirit" broadly. Such a woman may well raise her voice or perform her tasks with vigor. But she has learned to be tranquil inside in the face of all circumstances. She exemplifies the fruit of the Holy Spirit as a well-cared-for fruit tree might do, bearing fruit season after season, never straining to change from a golden delicious apple to a blushing peach. The woman who walks in the Spirit, regardless of the arrangement of her physical features, is beautiful.

A woman's physical beauty will deteriorate and fade with age, but her inner beauty will become more beautiful as she matures in Christ. I have known godly women whose physical bodies were crippled and deformed, but whose beautiful inner walk made them beautiful to behold.

Discipline your body

A woman who is Christ-controlled will have access to the power that will help her lead a disciplined life. She will not undereat or overeat, she will be as fit as possible without letting fitness rule her thoughts, and she will quickly return to equilibrium when something throws her off balance. She will enjoy intervals of Sabbath rest and hard labor. She will spend time reading the Word, praying, and serving others. Her commitment to let God's will be accomplished in her life will affect her attitudes, actions, and reactions.

Her life will be an invitation to His life—"Come on in; the Water [of Life] is fine!"

WIFE AS MOTHER

We cannot leave our discussion of a Spirit-empowered woman without touching on her role as a mother and teacher of her children. Even women who do not have children discover that they have a nurturing side, and God will show them how to fulfill their desire to create and foster new life.

For years, a mother's primary role is that of servant. Nine months of waiting for the blessed event are rewarded with sleepless nights, mountains of laundry, and strictly curbed liberty. Many young mothers feel like prisoners in their own homes. Then at last, the little helpless babe rewards Mom for all her efforts with a half smile. That sets the stage for an endless cycle of serving and rewards.

If she doesn't watch out, a mother can become so involved in her baby's life that her marriage suffers. Her husband may or may not be able to articulate his feeling of neglect. Some time ago, I heard a sermon in which the minister stated that a baby could be either a "blessing or a blight." Ironically, he noted, young couples pray fervently for a baby. Then when that prayer is answered, the newborn can become a wedge between the father and mother and even between the parents and God. Spiritually bankrupt, such parents start their son or daughter down the wrong path before they realize what they're doing. Within that small child's body is the capacity to become a full-grown man or woman who will become part of the kingdom of God. God delights to convert our "blights" into "blessings"—after all, He sent a baby when He had a job to accomplish, and His name was Jesus!

"Children are a heritage from the LORD, the fruit of the womb is a reward" (Ps. 127:3). I can just hear some of you young mothers sighing with disagreement because at the moment, your children seem to be more of a punishment than a reward. After you've spent the night walking the floor with a howling infant or after you've heard that your child is failing in all his classes or has become addicted to drugs, you would just as soon trade in your so-called reward for some personal peace.

And yet children are a gift from God, custom-tailored for their parents. The daunting task of rearing a child teaches us new degrees of unselfishness and persistence. All that hard work pays off, if we do it in the Spirit (looking to Him for strength and wisdom and endeavoring to be as obedient as we can). Our children may rebel later in their lives, but if we have tried to follow God's instruction book (the Word), we will have given them the best possible foundation for living.

Follow the instructions

One year we gave our sons a Christmas gift of an elaborate Erector Set. Our boys enjoyed the gift, creating many clever designs—because they followed the instructions. Now Erector Sets don't have free wills as human beings do, so the results of our parental care don't always turn out looking like the pictures. Sometimes, they turn out marred beyond recognition. But that doesn't make the instruction book wrong.

One of the most thumbed through portions of my Bible is the Book of Proverbs. That book contains more advice for raising and training children than any other book in the Bible. As I brought up my children, I went there first for all my child-rearing advice. For example:

> Trust in the LORD with all thine heart; and lean not unto thine own understanding. In all thy ways acknowledge him, and he shall direct thy paths.
> —PROVERBS 3:5–6, KJV

> The rod of correction imparts wisdom, but a child left to himself disgraces his mother.
> —PROVERBS 29:15, NIV

It's from the Bible that I learned how to calm my frantic heart when circumstances were beyond my control: "Thou wilt keep him in perfect peace, whose mind is stayed on thee: because he trusteth in thee" (Isa. 26:3, KJV). The Word taught me that I didn't have to be afraid to be in charge of my children. (See Hebrews 12.) Children need to know that someone is stronger and more capable than they are. Even if they protest against your discipline, deep inside they feel more secure when they see you exercising your parental authority: "He who ignores discipline despises himself, but whoever heeds correction gains understanding" (Prov. 15:32, NIV).

Although I see many mistakes when I look back on my child-rearing years, I also see that God honors a mother and father who put Him first. He covered many of our mistakes and made the best of others. Now it is our prayer that our children will teach these same biblical principles to their children and train them up in the way they should go. We may not have been perfect examples for them, but certainly they were raised on biblical principles right out of the best instruction book in the world.

Parents united
Probably some of our most heartbreaking counseling sessions have been with mothers and fathers who had failed to agree about the

teaching and discipline of their children. As the passing years uncovered the fact that their division had produced havoc and despair, they would bare their troubled hearts to us. Usually, it was too late to make effective changes.

Young parents would avoid some of the trauma of rebellious children if they would agree at the beginning to be united in administering discipline. It is essential that they work together as a team. Children catch on very young when Mom and Dad do not agree with each other, and they begin to play one parent against the other. They also recognize early if their parents do not follow through on their threats. Without becoming harsh and heartless, parents can be firm and consistent and fair, coming to God often for more wisdom and insight.

Much of a mother's job description turns out to be a teaching responsibility. Although Ephesians 6 instructs fathers to oversee the discipline and instruction of the children, the mother, as the help-meet, has a giant share in this project. Usually spending many more waking hours with the children than their father does, she carries out standards that they have agreed upon together.

Wife First, Mother Second

After the children are grown, the wife and husband may live alone together for thirty years or more. This means that about half of the average marriage will be spent without children. So the husband and wife had better be friends! We all know couples who have divorced after the age of forty, largely because they drifted apart during the child-rearing years.

When a young mother spends most of her time with the children, especially when their needs consume her every day, her husband may go his own way. Too often, the wife doesn't even notice.

Just as often, it's the husband who has started to drift. If his career keeps him away from home much of the time, the wife can start to feel like a single parent. Feeling trapped, she may yield to bitterness and self-pity. It can be very difficult for her, even if she has accepted the fact that she has "married his profession."

When you pray together as a couple, ideally you will pray for each other in turn and also for your marriage. God will never fail to honor your heartfelt prayers. He is more interested in the long-term success of your marriage than you realize. Jesus once told the Pharisees, "'For this reason a man will leave his father and mother and be united to his wife, and the two will become one flesh.' So they are no longer two, but one. Therefore what God has joined together, let man not separate" (Mark 10:7–9, NIV).

SPIRITUAL POWER FOR YOUR FAMILY: PRAYER

(Prayer of a Spirit-empowered wife)

> Lord in heaven, I know that You created marriage on earth to reflect Your relationship with Your people. Your church is Your bride just as I am my husband's bride.
>
> I ask You to be my sole source of wisdom and strength to be the best wife I can possibly be. Carry me through the difficult times with my love intact. Let my husband's trust in me be well placed and for his benefit. May our children rise up and call me blessed (happy) because of all You have done for me. And long after our children have gone away from home to start their own homes, may I still be the only woman my husband will ever desire.
>
> I put myself into Your capable hands today and every day for as long as I live. In the precious name of Jesus my Lord, amen.

CHAPTER 7

Becoming a Spirit-Empowered Husband

IF THE AUTOMOTIVE industry operated the way most people do today, rejecting all basic guidelines for life and believing that each generation must find for itself the best way to live, we would still be in the Model T age. I am sure that is why the average family suffers from unhappiness—the members of the family are stumbling around, trying to figure out the right way to operate.

Spirit-filled men and women do not need to stumble in the dark. Between the Bible and the Word living within us, we have an abundance of guidance. We have been considering God's Word to women in the past two chapters. Now let's turn our attention to husbands. As we did in our discussion of wives, we will examine some of our preconceived notions about the *man of the house* and hold them up against the Word of God to see what difference the Holy Spirit can make in a man's life and home.

Would you say that the term "Spirit-empowered husband" is a contradiction in terms? Perhaps it only applies to pastors or to men who are by nature more "touchy-feely"? Can it fit with our images of Iron Man masculinity or (more commonly) Mr. Joe Average?

Let's not let our limited experience hold us back from a full understanding of what it means to be a true man complete in all his facets— physical, mental, emotional, *and* spiritual. Let's not settle for married life that is little better than being "undivorced," living together in the same house with unresolved tensions that threaten to unravel the family fabric. It's not easy to allow the Holy Spirit to mold us into God's image. However, whom the Son makes free is free indeed. When we have been liberated from the prison of our unredeemed human nature, learning how to manage our sin rather than letting it manage us, we cast off the sense of failure and the frustration that were meant only to be temporary motivations to make us seek the help of the Spirit.

THE HUSBAND AS LEADER

God's first assignment for husbands is to be the leaders of their wives. Ephesians 5:23–27 (NIV) clearly states:

> For the husband is the head of the wife as Christ is the head of the church, his body, of which he is the Savior. Now as the church submits to Christ, so also wives should submit to their husbands in everything.
>
> Husbands, love your wives, just as Christ loved the church and gave himself up for her to make her holy, cleansing her by the washing with water through the word, and to present her to himself as a radiant church, without stain or wrinkle or any other blemish, but holy and blameless.

This matches Genesis 3:16, where God says to Eve, "Your desire shall be for your husband, and he shall rule over you." The principle is repeated in 1 Corinthians 11:3: "But I want you to know that the head of every man is Christ, the head of woman is man, and the head of Christ is God."

In the "Book of Beginnings," Genesis, where God laid out the tracks of life for people to run on, one of His foundational principles was that a woman's basic internal inclination would be to follow a man. When a man opens his life, home, and possessions to her, her natural response is to commit herself to him. If he shirks the role of leadership out of neglect, ignorance (because he did not see such a role exemplified by his father or does not know the Bible), or personal weakness, he condemns his wife to a lifetime of frustration. In all likelihood, she will become increasingly dominating, neurotic, or obnoxious. She finds it all but impossible to submit to a man who refuses to lead.

Whenever we talk about male leadership in the home, we tend to equate it with the old European, paternalistic family in which the father was a virtual dictator. Such a view does not coincide with biblical teaching. In the passage from Ephesians above, we see that God (who is love incarnate) gives us such an improved system that surely we should all realize we cannot achieve it without supernatural assistance. The husband is to serve as leader of the wife *as Christ is the head of the church*. Just as God has demonstrated His loving lordship to us, so husbands should shoulder their responsibilities in a spirit of love, always maintaining a supreme interest in the good of their wives and children.

The difference is simple. Without God's love, men become dictators—or they abdicate. In either case, they make selfish or unwise decisions. But with God's love informing their minds and flowing through their hearts, they can make even the most difficult decisions well, asking themselves, "In whose best interest is this decision being made? Mine?" Since men are only human, they may not always be right, but their motivation will come from the heart of God if they surrender to His lordship.

When Paul wrote, "Wives, submit to your own husbands, as to the Lord" (Eph. 5:22), please notice that the next sentence does *not* read, "Husbands, order your wives around." What he did write is this incomparable statement: "Husbands, love your wives, just as Christ also loved the church and gave Himself for her" (v. 25). Jesus Christ entered the world, not to serve His own interests, but to lay down His life for His people. He wants husbands to lay their lives down for the sake of their wives.

You would think that in our society, where independence is prized so highly, this approach to marriage wouldn't work anymore. But it does, because the principles of God's kingdom are eternal. Instead of being a patronizing way for a man to treat a woman, it parallels our Lord's self-sacrificing, ardent love.

This does not put the woman down, but rather it elevates her to her full and godly womanhood. We can compare a husband to a company president. He must be in charge of at least one employee, and quite possibly that employee (in this case, his wife) is his equal and possibly his superior in terms of intellect, character, and energy. Andrew Carnegie used to boast that his success could not have come from his personal skills alone, but should be attributed to the fact that he had hired subordinates who were more capable than he was. Would such an administrator dictate over superior people? Not at all. To gain their greatest productivity, he will allow them as much freedom as possible within the company structure, always considering their opinions when making decisions. In a much lesser fashion I can relate to that. As the chairman and founder of Concerned Women for America, I have men and women working for me with far greater skills than I have. Even though I am the final decision-maker, I certainly listen and consider their opinions and ideas. Similarly, a wise husband will take the feelings and opinions of his wife seriously. Concurring with her arguments in no way lessens his leadership.

Walking in the Spirit

Too often, men learn very little from their mistakes or the mistakes of others, which means they miss one of the most common training methods used by the Holy Spirit. The Lord wants us to "get it," and He will keep trying to get our attention. If you are a husband and father, look for His grace in action, teaching you how to walk in the Spirit.

A mature, Spirit-empowered husband will find that he operates according to the following guidelines:

1. He always prays for the decision-making wisdom that God promises to provide. (See James 1:5.)

2. He never makes a decision without hearing and evaluating his wife's views.

3. He always checks his motivation. "Is it really for the good of my wife and family, or could it be inspired by selfishness or prejudice? Do I feel any 'check' in my spirit about this?"

4. He uses tact in executing his decision, and if it is an unpopular one, he makes an effort not to alienate the family he loves.

5. Once the decision is made, he does not give in to pressure from anger, pouting, or resistance.

6. However, he is always open to further evidence that might render his original decision obsolete and warrant a change. A godly leader is flexible.

Leadership is not easy to maintain, and decision making becomes more complex as the family grows. At times, it can become downright lonely. But that's part of the job. As the heads of their homes, God holds husbands accountable to be obedient to His leadership even as they exercise theirs over their wives and families.

THE OTHER SIDE OF SUBMISSION

From a woman's perspective, it is not easy to submit to a man "in everything." A husband can help her by being fair, carefully attending to his wife's point of view and accepting it whenever possible. Sometimes her suggestions are more practical than his, and a man who is secure in his leadership role will be glad to see that.

In our case, I usually take longer to make a decision than my husband. When I eventually make up my mind, it often turns out that my slow processing has resulted in better judgment. Tim learned long ago not to pressure me into quick decisions; my response was to throw ice water on anything that he thrust upon me too suddenly. Before we were living a Spirit-filled life, he would press for my compliance, and I would respond by dragging my feet. He soon learned that his tactics left much to be desired. He had to adapt his leadership to my temperament. Once he factored that in, he discovered that he did not have to forfeit his leadership, and I found that my submission did not have to come at the expense of my self-respect.

Two Spirit-filled people will not experience total agreement—that's guaranteed. Tim and I see almost everything differently. Before a vacation, Tim likes to pack at the last minute, and then, as we're backing the car out of the driveway to embark on a three-thousand-mile trip, he asks me, "Would you look in the glove compartment and see if you can find a map?" I'm the type who visits the automobile club two months in advance to plan the route. Our differences show in all our decisions, from breakfast cereal to wallpaper. We used to be more surprised when we happened to agree than we were when we disagreed! However, now after many years of marriage, we find that our opinions are more and more alike.

Our differences don't mean we need to fight. We can *agree to disagree* (and agree to not chafe about it). We can resolve to *pray about it*. And—best of all—we can *ask the Holy Spirit for wisdom*. God has promised to give us wisdom when we ask, and we have found that He really does.

> If any of you lacks wisdom, he should ask God, who gives generously to all without finding fault, and it will be given to him.... The wisdom that comes from heaven is first of all pure; then peace-loving, considerate, submissive, full of mercy and good fruit, impartial and sincere.
>
> —JAMES 1:5; 3:17, NIV

CALLED TO SERVE

A husband is called to lay down his life in service to his wife. (See again Ephesians 5:23, 25–27, and also John 15:13.) This is basic to the Christian way of life. "Whosoever will be chief among you, let him be your servant" (Matt. 20:27, KJV). Far from *lording it over* the wife and children, a Spirit-directed husband will be tireless in his efforts to present his wife "holy and blameless" before God (Eph. 5:27, NIV).

If the man makes the first surrender to the Lord Jesus, all the rest of his family can find their way to a living faith by his example. As the head of the family, he represents his family to God. He prays for them regularly, and sometimes in their hearing. He establishes and maintains the family prayer times. As his wife and children hear him carrying the family concerns to their Father in heaven, they know a level of security that cannot be achieved in any other way.

A wise husband knows that becoming a Christian won't make him or anybody else in his family automatically treat each other faultlessly. He will redirect blame-casting and distrust by bringing the guilty parties to the foot of the cross and standing there with them, helping each member of his family recognize that we all need a Savior and that every one of us is utterly dependent upon His freely given love and forgiveness.

Such a husband and father will never need to bludgeon his family into submission. He doesn't have to insist on his own way. (See 1 Corinthians 13:5.) His wife and children can see that he wants them to become their own persons, and they are secure in the knowledge that Daddy won't resort to force or browbeating to make them behave. He won't manipulate them; he respects the free will of each individual in his household unless, in his mature wisdom, he sees danger and possible destruction in what they want to do. Then, because he is the loving head of the household, he will do all he can to rescue them and turn them around.

A Spirit-controlled man recognizes that God wants him to bless and fulfill his wife's life. It never crosses his mind to give up on his marriage because "she doesn't satisfy me." His wholehearted intent is *giving* instead of receiving—and yet, of course, he will find that his giving will rebound in measureless satisfaction for him.

THE FAMILY PROVIDER

From the very beginning, the man was given the responsibility of being the family breadwinner. God said to Adam, "In the sweat of your face you shall eat bread" (Gen. 3:19). Ever since, God has held the man accountable for both the material provision and the protection of his family.

Our human flesh is susceptible to Satan's temptation to laziness. God will not supply us with everything on a silver platter. The divine command to Adam is still in effect; man is to earn his bread by the sweat of his brow. Through the years, Tim and I have noticed that every time we asked God to supply a special need for our family, He answered by giving Tim some extra work that brought in additional income. Rarely did His answer come like manna from heaven.

In the New Testament, men are taught: "But if anyone does not provide for his own, and especially for those of his household, he has denied the faith and is worse than an unbeliever" (1 Tim. 5:8). Whenever a husband fails to be the primary breadwinner in his marriage, this deficiency becomes a serious threat to his role of leadership, not to mention to his personal self-esteem. Of course there are temporary exceptions to this, such as when the husband is in school or training and he and his wife agree that she will work to support them. Or, early in their marriage before babies arrive, they decide that the young wife will work to help build a nest egg for when she begins to stay home with the children. But this shouldn't be a permanent way of life. As a basic rule of thumb, the husband's job should earn enough to provide food, shelter, and clothing. If the wife works outside the home when the children are in school, her income should pay for the extras such as a house down payment, tuition for the children to attend a Christian school or college tuition, furniture, or purchases that the husband's income cannot provide. Unfortunately, if the husband cannot provide enough for the family to live, it often is the children who will be set aside with substitute care while the mother goes to work.

A man needs the sense of responsibility that comes with knowing that his family is depending on him for the necessities of life. One of the dreadful results of our country's welfare system is that the welfare subsidies can be higher than the wages for unskilled labor, which can strip able-bodied men of their self-respect.

The highly technological nature of the workplace today has complicated man's role as provider. Often the husband must undertake specialized training, and couples must delay starting a family longer than they would like. Ever-present inflation further complicates the situation by putting house buying beyond the reach of average newlyweds. Despite these serious impediments, a Christian husband should make every effort, if he is physically able to do so, to provide for his wife and children.

BALANCING THE SPIRITUAL AND THE MATERIAL

The Spirit-filled family provider will not be a lazy man, nor will he be obsessed with obtaining material goods. Instead, he will "seek first the kingdom of God and His righteousness, and all these things shall be added to [him]" (Matt. 6:33).

There is nothing wrong with a Christian man's interest in business success. But when his interest in business overshadows his love for spiritual things, he and his family are in trouble. In our society, this is so common as to appear to be normal. The Christian man who hides behind his work to avoid cultivating his spiritual or family life is not Spirit-controlled—he's a self-driven workaholic. A Spirit-controlled husband and father may work hard and may endure periods of heavy work pressure, but his work does not take priority over his family.

I don't believe that we need to become obsessed with "keeping the Sabbath" strictly, but I do believe that God will provide wisdom to make it possible not to work every Sunday. I watched one man make the mistake of working every Sunday. He was a manager of a super-market, and he made double-time pay for Sunday work. He justified it because he felt his family needed the money. So he rarely went to church, although he assured everyone that he "loved the Lord." His underdeveloped spiritual life and poor example caused his three daughters to grow up with very little interest in God, and they married men who had even less interest. The last I knew, he was upset because his wife was seeing another man. What an expensive price to pay for double-time wages!

Then I think of another man who was a physician in a small town. His patient load was staggering. After a full day of seeing patients in his office, he would remain "on call" through the night. In addition, he was obligated to visit a number of his patients every day in the local hospital. But instead of going straight from the office to the hospital, which would have been expedient for him, every single day he chose to come home to his wife and family for dinner, saving his hospital visits for later in the evening. His wife and children knew they could "have his ear" at that time of day (although sometimes he was so tired he fell asleep sitting at the table!). Moreover, on his one day off each week, he took his wife on a "date day." It was special for both of them, even if all they did was take a long walk and then go to the local hardware store to buy light bulbs. About once a month, this man took one of his three children out of school so the child could have time alone with him on the day off, enjoying a special day that could include shopping, a sports event, a movie, or lunch at a favorite restaurant.

THE FAMILY PROTECTOR

As far back as anthropologists go in their research, the man has always been the protector of his family. We visited Africa years ago, where we saw a typical native scene: a small village of five huts, all surrounded by a handmade wall with only one gate. At the gate sat the father, bow across his lap, plainly there to protect the homes of his five wives and twenty-nine children.

Our need for physical protection won't be the same, but here are a few of the ways that we should understand the husband's role in our society:

He will protect his wife psychologically.

What a wife thinks of herself influences everything she does. In fact, it's more important than what she supposes other people think of her. Her husband's opinion of her is of paramount importance. If he approves of her, it matters little who does not. But if he does not esteem her, it does not matter who else does.

The Bible tells us that a husband should "honor...the wife as...the weaker vessel" (1 Pet. 3:7). In the negative, this means that he will refrain from putting her down, especially in public. He will find ways to praise her. Even if she is doing nearly everything wrong, the Holy Spirit can help him find positive things to say to her.

One of the secondary meanings for the biblical word *submission* involves being a "responder." A woman responds to her husband. Of course she will respond more favorably to love, kindness, and praise.

Conversely, she feels confused and vulnerable if she has nothing, or very little, to respond to. She finds mental and emotional security, and a strong sense of teamwork, when she can share her husband's thoughts. If he has a shallow commitment to Jesus, she rightfully feels uncovered and endangered. If she overhears him tell someone else a new idea that he hasn't yet mentioned to her, she feels betrayed or even railroaded, especially if he presents the idea as if it represents their agreed-upon viewpoint.

Unfortunately, if a husband believes that he cannot trust his wife, this pattern will perpetuate itself. She needs to honor confidences and share her thoughts with him as well.

He will protect his children psychologically.

Same song, second verse. No man looms larger in the hearts of his children than their father does. Consequently, what he thinks of them is of crucial significance in their formative years. He may need to learn to gear down to their level to make sure his praises hit the mark, but nothing will nurture them better than sincere and frequent doses of vitamin "E" (encouragement).

Praises may be related to achievements, but the underlying message expressed should focus on character traits. "I'm so proud of you for scoring the winning goal, but I'd be just as pleased if you hadn't because of the way you treated the members of the losing team." Through it all, the father should give verbal and physical expression to his unconditional love for each child. He can't just assume the child knows he's loved. Hugs and "I love you's" should be frequent and sincere.

He will protect his family from philosophical error.

Our world has become a battleground for the control of the human mind. Every Christian father should be awake to the situation. Through his Spirit-directed conduct in his home, his decisions, his reliance on the Bible, and the positive, informed influence of others, a husband and father can equip his family to live holy lives that will bear fruit now and in eternity.

The attractions of TV, the Internet, movies, books, and magazines are powerful. Our school system has deteriorated to the point that our children can be brainwashed with evil philosophies—unless they have internal resources from home as weapons. A father may be able to send his children to a Christian school or, with his wife, homeschool them, but even so, the sounds of battle will remain clearly audible.

He will protect his wife and children from disrespect.

Disrespect starts within the walls of home. At first, it usually takes the form of children's insubordination to their mother. If not stopped early, it becomes a bad pattern that only a father can cure. If he does not, he will find it turned against him and the values he taught, then against society, and finally possibly against the law.

Assuming he and his wife express respect for each other, it should be fairly instinctive for a man to recognize and stand in the way of disrespect when it comes from his children's mouths. Tim tells a true story about his father, who had only an eighth-grade education but who had no trouble teaching his son how to respect his mother. One day when Tim was in the fourth grade, he came home from school and addressed his mother in a sassy and disrespectful manner. He hadn't realized his father was already home. Suddenly he heard his name called from the next room. He slunk in to stand before his father, who said sternly, "Young man, I want you to go back into the kitchen and apologize to your mother. And if I ever hear you speak to her again that way, there will be a hole in the wall just your size!" Tim got the message, loud and clear. His mother lived to be eighty-one years old, and she never heard him speak disrespectfully to her again as long as she lived!

A SPIRIT-FILLED TEMPERAMENT

As we have seen in chapters five and six, each temperament type has special challenges—and particular rewards. Here is a brief overview of the four primary temperament types as they can be applied to husbands:

Melancholic

A man who is primarily melancholic will be a deep thinker with great sensitivity. His is the most gifted of the temperaments, but underneath he often feels inferior. He cannot handle criticism well. A melancholic man may look for a wife for a long time; he is idealistic and wants his wife to measure up to a high standard. Once he is married, he tends to be a legalistic nitpicker. One might think he would be able to find something to criticize even if he could revert his family to measuring up to the pharisaical laws of the Old Testament. However, with the Spirit's help, he can become a leader known for his *sweet reasonableness*.

Phlegmatic

A man who is predominantly phlegmatic is an introvert, as is his melancholic brother. He is pleasant to live with, and he won't purposely stir up emotional storms. In fact, he dislikes conflict and will tend to withdraw from it. He will need to ask the Holy Spirit to help him become a more aggressive leader in his home. He prefers to go off by himself and putter instead of spending time with his wife and children. He may hold his possessions too closely, not wanting to loan them to others. As a child, he may have found satisfaction in teasing others, and as a man he may not have outgrown this tendency. He will give advice when asked, but his reserved nature may intimidate others to the point that they are afraid to ask. He is not a natural leader, which may create problems in his marriage if his wife possesses an assertive personality. But he will be a quiet, stable *anchor* in his home, and by example, he will teach his children a commonsense approach to life.

Choleric

Although a choleric man is definitely a strong natural leader, he will need to ask the Holy Spirit to help him develop compassion for his family members and others. He has been hard-driving and independent from his youth, and he has grown up expecting people to follow him readily and work hard. *Submission* seems like a foreign concept to him, and he may need some hard knocks in his married life before he realizes that he needs to submit his free will to the lordship of Jesus. The choleric husband will be admirably determined and persistent; he will not rest until a problem is solved. If he surrenders his strengths to God, he will truly exemplify a man after God's own heart.

Sanguine

A sanguine husband and father is a pleasant fellow to have around. He may not be a deep thinker, but who cares? Even his inconsistent leadership is easy to forgive, although sometimes he is too quick to make impossible decisions, which he expects his wife to execute. He will enjoy spending time with his wife and children and will look for ways to include them in his favorite activities. His inborn restlessness will tend to sabotage the success of difficult projects. He's on the moody side, singing merrily in the car one moment, and furious at the driver who cut him off the next—then remorseful for his outburst. At least he finds it relatively easy to repent, he will need to ask forgiveness on a regular basis to keep walking in the Spirit.

As I noted in chapter five, you can find additional resources to help you explore and fine-tune your understanding of temperament types. I don't want to get sidetracked by devoting too much of this particular book to this topic, although, obviously, human personality traits have huge implications for marriage and family life.

Don't miss the significance of the bottom line, which applies equally to men and women. Look at each temperament combination as it is represented in your own family, and ask the Holy Spirit to show you the difference between traits that He is in the process of redeeming and traits that remain merely human. Even *good* traits need His touch. If we claim to belong wholly to the Lord Jesus, our lives will manifest more and more of His love.

God loves variety, and He made each one of us unique. What better way can we respond to Him than to give Him our whole selves?

SPIRITUAL POWER FOR YOUR FAMILY: PRAYER

My Lord and Savior,
I confess that I have not thought deeply about being a better husband and father. I thought it was just one of those things all men learn as they go through life.

I want to have more of Your help now that I know some of the areas in which I need it. It's obvious to me that I can't pull myself up by my own bootstraps; this business of loving my wife as You loved the church will occupy me for the rest of my days. I need every bit of spiritual assistance You can supply.

I pray that You will keep me sensitive to Your voice, and that even as I experience Your correction, You will also encourage me. You are my Lord and my God.

In Jesus' holy name, amen.

CHAPTER 8

Husband as Lover, Husband as Father

NEVER FORGET—IT is impossible to live according to the Word of God apart from the power of the Holy Spirit. All of the advice Paul gives to husbands and wives in Ephesians 5:22–6:4 is given within the context of that truth. Look at the verses that he placed just before he wrote his advice for couples and families:

> Therefore be imitators of God as dear children. And walk in love, as Christ also has loved us and given Himself for us.... But fornication and all uncleanness or covetousness, let it not even be named among you, as is fitting for saints; neither filthiness, nor foolish talking, nor coarse jesting, which are not fitting, but rather giving of thanks.... Walk as children of light (for the fruit of the Spirit is in all goodness, righteousness, and truth), finding out what is

acceptable to the Lord.... Therefore He says: "Awake, you who sleep, arise from the dead, and Christ will give you light." See then that you walk circumspectly, not as fools but as wise, redeeming the time, because the days are evil. Therefore do not be unwise, but understand what the will of the Lord is. And do not be drunk with wine, in which is dissipation; but be filled with the Spirit, speaking to one another in psalms and hymns and spiritual songs, singing and making melody in your heart to the Lord, giving thanks always for all things to God the Father in the name of our Lord Jesus Christ.

—EPHESIANS 5:1–4, 8–10, 14–20

These verses provide a wealth of practical help for walking in the Spirit successfully. They help to keep us growing in our lives in Christ Jesus as we move through each day of our married lives. Paul boldly presents *must-dos* in these verses, important guidelines for the Spirit-controlled man (or woman).

1. Be imitators of God (v. 1).
2. Walk in love (v. 2).
3. Don't even mention anything unholy (vv. 3–4).
4. Give thanks (v. 4).
5. Walk as children of light (v. 8).
6. Find out what is acceptable to the Lord (v. 10).
7. Walk circumspectly (cautiously, prudently) (v. 15).
8. Be wise; understand God's will (v. 17).
9. Do not be drunk with wine (v. 18).
10. Be filled with the Spirit (v. 18).
11. Speak to others in psalms and songs (v. 19).
12. Make melody in your heart to the Lord (v. 19).
13. Give thanks always for all things (v. 20).

With our willing cooperation and the ongoing help of His Holy Spirit, we can become more peaceful and more joyful in the context of living with our spouses and children.

THE HUSBAND AS IDEAL LOVER

Following God, the greatest love in a man's life should be his wife. After all, in Matthew 19:19, a man is commanded to love his neighbor only as he loves himself, but in Ephesians 5:25, he is told to love his wife as Christ loved the church, which is to say he should love her with complete self-sacrifice.

No emotion is more needed or more talked about—and less understood—than love. Poems have been written about it; stories, plays, and movies have portrayed it; people never seem to tire of hearing about it. Yet except for mother love, very few of us experience the reality of the expression of true love.

True husband-wife love is supernatural, a result of being filled with the Spirit of God. That kind of love is a treasure that grows and matures through the years. It does not depend on a single event. It requires a lifetime to express. As a man and a woman share their total selves unconditionally, their love can absorb conflict, disagreement, disappointment, tragedy, and selfishness. Their love is to their marriage what shock absorbers are to a car—a strong cushion for the rough spots in life. True love does not require two perfect people, but it does require two people who are filled with and wholly dependent upon the Holy Spirit. A husband who nurtures this kind of love is guaranteed a steady return on his investment. (See Galatians 6:7–8.)

WHAT DOES LOVE DO?

It is self-evident that married love includes a sexual relationship. Often, unfortunately, far too much of the response to the question "What does love do?" centers around techniques for enhancing sexual pleasure. But it takes a lot more than skillful performance in the bedroom to achieve a satisfying love life. Sex in marriage is very important, but it is only part of the overall love relationship.

We can learn the most about what love does by considering the familiar words of 1 Corinthians 13:4–8 (NIV):

> Love is patient, love is kind. It does not envy, it does not
> boast, it is not proud. It is not rude, it is not self-seeking,
> it is not easily angered, it keeps no record of wrongs. Love
> does not delight in evil but rejoices with the truth. It always
> protects, always trusts, always hopes, always perseveres.
> Love never fails. But where there are prophecies, they will
> cease; where there are tongues, they will be stilled, where
> there is knowledge, it will pass away.

True love is patient (v. 4).

Many translators use the word *longsuffering* here. This kind of love
will accept slights and rebuffs lovingly and without retaliation.

A husband will learn to restrain the "wild horses" of his passions,
remembering that his beloved needs a steady flow of loving expressions in the form of physical touches, smiles, words, and countless
little gestures. Loving patience wins her over.

How do you respond to your wife before and during her menstrual
period? She may be less lovable at that time. A wise husband anticipates that time of month (and any of his wife's other particular pressure points) and goes out of his way to show his love regardless of her
response.

True love is kind (v. 4).

To a woman, kindness is the most important expression of love.
A woman may be able to endure crushing pain bravely, but she will
remain vulnerable to unkindness from her husband or children.

Most men do not realize that just as they are stimulated visually,
their wives respond to verbal cues. Whether he realizes it or not,
a man who comes in the door barking out criticism, demands, and
insults is committing sexual suicide. Contrast him to the lover who,
motivated by love and respect for his wife, comes through the door
with kind words and tender speech. His love expresses itself in a host
of thoughtful gestures that are meaningful to a wife.

But what turns one woman on may be insignificant to another. A happy husband will find out his wife's "love language." For example, I happen to love flowers—real ones, or second best, silk ones. If Tim had his way, he would substitute plastic flowers because he says they are so much easier to take care of, and they last longer than cut flowers. There is just one thing wrong with that idea: I hate plastic flowers. Consequently, Tim brings me fresh flowers on a regular basis. It's one of the ways I know he loves me.

True love is generous.

Generosity is the rich soil in which the roots of other qualities of love can best grow. A generous husband takes genuine delight in his partner's successes. He is secure, and he loves to see his wife's finer qualities outshine his. His generosity will spill over into the way he and his wife spend money, entertain, and donate to charitable causes.

Love is giving, and the true lover knows that the best way to get love is to give it away.

True love is humble (v. 4).

Pride is the greatest single enemy any man faces. Like a roaring lion, Satan undermines a man's true strength by appealing to his pride. (See 1 Peter 5:8.) A proud spirit is a destroyer of true love; therefore, it has no place in the life of a Spirit-controlled husband, whose love inspires him to forget himself and his *rights* in deference to the needs of his wife and family.

In the old days, there was a clear-cut separation between *his* duties and *hers*. The wife was responsible for everything that went on inside the house, and the man took care of everything outside. Now that the 140 acres outside have shrunk to a garage and a patch of grass, there should be plenty of time to help the wife with the after-dinner dishes, take care of the children, and even change a diaper or two. Instead of filling his garage with power tools or sports equipment, the Spirit-inspired husband will think also of his wife, whose "work is never done." If a wife has to work outside the home, her husband's in-house chores will increase. When a wife is expecting, or after the baby arrives, it is again a loving tribute to her when the husband willingly assumes some of her chores. Husbands, you have not abdicated your responsibility as head of the home by helping to fulfill your wife's duties.

True love is polite (v. 5).

Electronic door openers and other mechanical contrivances, along with the self-sufficient tone of our times, do nothing to cultivate courtesy and polite behavior. Many a man no longer opens doors for his wife or remembers on which side of the sidewalk to escort her. Women, of course, are quite capable of opening their own doors, but men need to remember these gestures of respect. Women of all ages enjoy being treated as someone special.

True love is unselfish (v. 5).

Selfishness devours marital happiness. Love erases selfishness and self-seeking. Spirit-controlled love will look for ways to express itself.

Every couple has different tastes. Tim is a sports nut, and I love the symphony and opera. To better love Tim, I have cultivated a genuine interest in athletics. And although he'd almost rather have the proverbial root canal, Tim has, to his credit, escorted me to the concert hall as well.

True love is gracious (vv. 4–7).

The best-tempered homes will always be occupied by a Spirit-controlled couple. The gracious love and peace of the Holy Spirit will replace all disharmony, short tempers, and irritability. True love is not touchy, easily offended, or defensive. It never responds with angry hostility. Not that disruptions never happen, but with the love of God "in house," wise solutions and growing maturity will prevail.

"Husbands, love your wives and do not be harsh with them" (Col. 3:19, NIV). True love creates an environment of encouragement, where healthy deference and submission thrive. Such a husband never, ever has to demand respect or submission from his wife.

True love is trusting (v. 7).

Jealousy is a cruel taskmaster and an unnecessary bedfellow in a Spirit-controlled marriage. Usually generated by the insecurities of one partner more than by the deeds of the other, it is counter to true, trusting love. True love "thinks no evil." If you have a temperament that is easily given to critical or jealous thoughts, ask God to help you evaluate each situation through the magnifying glass of His love. A loving spirit not only goes the extra mile; it is also quick to excuse.

True love is sincere (v. 6).

Deceit is harmful to any relationship, but it is devastating in a marriage. Women who say "I cannot trust my husband" are all too common. Some wives cannot trust their husbands in any area—financial, moral, relational. An immoral man cannot be trusted in anything, because his sexual sins lead to lying, financial manipulations, and widespread deceit.

Remember Paul's caution in Ephesians 5:3–7, in which he makes it clear that all immoral, unclean, and dishonest behavior is forbidden. Paul says we shouldn't even talk about it—and he wrote his advice long before he knew what would one day be portrayed in the movies and television of our day!

True love goes out of its way to be honest in word and deed. This is never more apparent than after an argument. Love doesn't keep accounts or play one-upmanship. Instead, it hurries to the aid of the beloved and tries to rectify all misunderstandings. The Spirit-controlled husband will humbly confess his error not only to God but also to his wife or his children, as the occasion demands. God in His grace has granted us a merciful way of removing sins and injuries through sincere confession. Many a relationship has been spared needless pain by the simple but manly admission, "Honey, I was wrong, and I hope you will forgive me. I'm sorry I hurt you."

LOVE NEVER FAILS

You will find that the intensity of love will rise and fall, depending on the season of life, your spiritual condition, and the pressure of your vocation.

For a husband, heavy business pressures decrease his interest in lovemaking. In fact, surveys suggest that the more cerebral a man's job, the less frequent is his sexual desire. Those with the greatest desire are men with physical jobs or tasks most easily left at the place of employment at the end of the day.

But both men and women will find seasons when their love lives will be less than intense. A pastor with three sermons on Sunday morning and one or two on Sunday evening may function as a zero on Saturday nights. Salesmen in the midst of a campaign, professional men driving hard to finish a project, and wives during a time of illness or just before the annual visit of the in-laws may go through a dormant time. It's perfectly natural as long as it's not protracted. At such times, a good principle to keep in mind appears in 1 Corinthians 13:8: "Love never fails."

MAKE TIME FOR LOVE

The pressurized age in which we live seriously infringes upon our free time. In spite of our push-button appliances and time-saving electronic gadgetry, we have no more spare time available to us than did our forefathers.

Often husbands get in such a hurry that they have no time for love. Many wives share a pet peeve: "My husband holds down two jobs [or one job and thirteen hobbies] and has no time for me." Without realizing it, the husband's merry-go-round of activities has speeded up so much he can't stop it. A wise husband schedules some "couple time," occasional dinners out, or even mini-honeymoons. This is particularly helpful after the children arrive.

Tailor your outings to your budget, of course, but by all means have them. There is something exciting about a night in a motel without routine household distractions. It not only gives you a few hours to get reacquainted, but it also puts the mystery and spark back into your love life. To your wife, this says, "I love you, and I enjoy spending time with you."

REDEEMED LOVERS

Judging by the amount of "press" given to husbands in Ephesians 5, a husband's love is the one essential ingredient without which a Christian home will be merely another human household.

Men, your Savior wants you to know how you can become the best possible lover for your wife. Let's take a brief look at how the four basic temperament types influence a man's ability to love his wife:

If you are a *melancholy* husband, your capacity for showing kindness and passion to your wife is almost unlimited, and your ability to analyze and remember her preferences should enable you to become "king of the mountain" in your marriage—even though you may never quite feel sure that all is going well. One of your problems to work on is your melancholy criticism, which could keep you from showing kindness and passion to your wife. Ask the Lord to fill you with the love and gentleness that can overcome your critical ways, and your love life will be enriched.

If you are a *phlegmatic* husband, your natural kindheartedness and gentleness will make you a patient lover. However, your tendency to be a fearful person can also affect your love life. You can have a fear of rejection even though it may be unrealistic, and this could cause you to withdraw into yourself, which can damage your wife's confidence in you. She needs you to communicate with her. Ask the Holy Spirit to give you ideas and to help you initiate loving gestures. Pay a little more attention to your appearance than you are accustomed to doing. Otherwise, you may become as comfortable as an old shoe—and most wives don't find those very exciting. In general, though, you do well as a husband. Therefore, while so much marital advice seems to be for other men, be careful not to make yourself an exception to the universal requirement of seeking to be filled with the Spirit in all aspects of your personality.

If you are a *choleric* husband, emotionally, you are an extremist, fiery hot one moment (with passion or with anger) and cold as stone the next. Your sarcastic tongue can quickly *turn off* the wife you love, and your do-everything-quick attitude can be a real deterrent to the loving *lead time* your wife needs. Because cholerics tend to be workaholics, oftentimes you need to ask the Lord to motivate you to make your marriage as much a priority as a work project you are working on. Then your wife and your children are sure to benefit from your strong and passionate leadership.

If you are a *sanguine* husband, you are charming, responsive, and enthused about your love life, and your male ego is firmly attached to this aspect of your life. This will be a good thing if you make up your mind early to confine your enthusiasm to your wife alone (and to encourage her to reciprocate, which will keep you coming back to her). Otherwise, the *wandering eye* that goes along with your temperament may plunge you into trouble you will regret. Ask the Holy Spirit to help you channel your energy, enthusiasm, and thought life to stay on track.

HUSBAND AS FATHER

The first commandment God gave to Adam and Eve was, "Be fruitful and multiply; fill the earth" (Gen. 1:28). God invented fatherhood.

A father's love for his children is so important that without it, a curse comes upon the land. "And he [Elijah] shall turn the heart of the fathers to the children, and the heart of the children to their fathers, lest I come and smite the earth with a curse" (Mal. 4:6, KJV). The word applies to fathers, not to mothers or parents together, or to the children.

Fathers are important simply because God created them to be important. God Himself is a Father. Just as human beings have life because of their Father God, so children have life because of their fathers. I don't mean "life" merely in terms of conception...I mean *ongoing life*. Children draw their identity, security, and maturity from their fathers. Whenever a father hugs or disciplines his children, he conveys life to them. When he listens to them, comforts them, or explains something to them, he gives them some more life.

In recent years, modern science has put into the hands of young couples birth-control techniques that enable them to limit the size of their families and, in a surprising number of cases, avoid having children altogether. This contrasts with the words of the psalmist: "Children are a heritage from the LORD, the fruit of the womb is a reward. Like arrows in the hand of a warrior, so are the children of one's youth. Happy is the man who has his quiver full of them" (Ps. 127:3–5). An old Hebrew tradition says that a quiver that soldiers carried to the battlefield was large enough to contain five arrows. This may suggest that a man would be happiest with five children.

Of course, almost any man can propagate children, but bringing them up is a different matter. Fatherhood takes hard work, sacrifice, and time, but it holds a great reward.

THE NATURE OF FATHERHOOD

The Spirit-filled father does not lack specific instructions from the Word of God as to the true nature of his duties. Let's start with Ephesians 6:4, "And you, fathers, do not provoke your children to wrath, but bring them up in the training and admonition of the Lord." I want to separate the commands in this verse for our consideration.

1. Fathers, love your children.

This is the positive way of saying, "Do not provoke your children to wrath." Every child needs love and intuitively seeks it from his parents. If his love is rejected or if Mom and Dad do not exhibit affection, he is filled with wrath.

Anyone who knows anything about the juvenile scene today sees the hostility carried by teens, which corresponds to the high rate of rejection or negligence on the part of their parents, especially their fathers (since so many of them are raised by single mothers). A juvenile-court judge, after presiding over thousands of juvenile cases, observed, "I have yet to see a boy come before my court who had a father who took him fishing or went to ball games or spent time with him." The father who demonstrates his love for his children by making time for teaching them, no matter how busy his schedule, enjoys his children when they are adults.

Even the children of loving, Spirit-controlled fathers may manifest a degree of wrath at times, but the anger in their spirits will be much less severe and more short-lived than that of the child who has been deprived of his basic need for father-love.

2. Fathers, teach your children.

If there is a consistent neglect among fathers today, it is in taking their responsibility as teachers of their children. Because Mother is the primary teacher during the first few years of a youngster's life, many men never assume their proper teaching role when the children get older. Even in dedicated homeschooling families, the mother does most of the actual teaching.

The Scriptures clearly state that fathers are to bring up their children in the nurture of the Lord—that is, training them by example and discipline. By nature, children do not tell the truth, nor do they automatically share or act responsibly. These are principles that must be instilled by example and precept. In addition, children must be taught skills commensurate with their age and gender.

In the old days, life was simpler. A father had only a few tools, all of which his son could be taught to use at an early age. Although today's power equipment presents special problems, the children must learn, and Father is still their best resource. If he spends time teaching skills, sports, and social customs, his children will more readily listen when he imparts to them the principles of the character of God.

3. Fathers, discipline your children.

The hardest job in the whole business of fatherhood is discipline. Without it, men fail in their parenthood.

Discipline is not to be confused with abuse. We hear a great deal about child abuse. What would make an adult strike a helpless child? The answer: the frustration of rage in an undisciplined person. Usually himself the product of a rejecting or permissive home, the father cannot endure the pressure of endless crying or childish behavior. Few child-beaters are murderers at heart, but all are selfish, angry, undisciplined people who themselves were abused in childhood.

However, as tragic as that kind of child abuse may be, another variety is far more common and less publicized. Consider carefully the lack of parental discipline itself. This could be considered a form of abuse. Most penitentiaries, juvenile halls, houses of correction, and cemeteries are full of the products of such homes. Many other children grow up as borderline casualties. They may marry and divorce several times, father and abandon children, fail to keep a job. Such situations could have been avoided had their fathers heeded the biblical injunction to discipline their children.

If you are a product of an abusive home, and you see that you are perpetuating the same pattern, take a serious look at yourself and seek the help of a godly pastor or counselor who can give you biblical counseling. Trying to be free of this by yourself without the Lord's help will be difficult and almost impossible, but with the help of a godly counselor you can be set free. Most of all, don't ignore it and try to excuse it away. The Holy Spirit is able to bring new thoughts and actions into your life that will change your actions toward your family.

Self-discipline, self-denial, and self-control are absolute essentials for mature adulthood. A father cannot possibly prepare his children educationally or vocationally for all the complex changes that await them, but he can do one thing: he can teach them self-discipline. That will prepare them for any uncertainty.

What Will Your Children Say?

Sixteen Christians attending a home Bible study were asked the question, "What was your father like?"

One said, "He was a loving, tender guy."

Another commented that her dad was a dedicated Christian who loved her very much.

Some reported that they "never really knew" their dads, and so on around the room.

Not one person mentioned the father's profession, possessions, or position in life. This should tell us something.

What would your children say about you? You aren't impressing them with what you do for a living; they may not even know what you do for a living. You matter to them because of who you are. Who are you?

The Husband as Family Priest

The most neglected role of the husband is that of family priest. In Ephesians 5 we read that the husband is to the wife what Christ is to the church. If Jesus Christ is our high priest, then you, husband, are the priest of your home. All spiritual instruction is your responsibility, not to mention spiritual protection for your wife and family.

We all realize that in many homes the mother takes care of the religious training of the children during their early years, although most likely the children will forget much of what she has taught them when they reach their teens if the father has no interest in spiritual things. Children possess a distinct spiritual side to their nature that must be cultivated carefully. Far too many Christian fathers believe they have fulfilled their parental responsibility by providing food, shelter, love, and discipline for their children. But they neglect their spiritual potential. Fathers, lead your children in the paths of the Lord.

Consider the following ways you fulfill your role as family priest:

1. You will be a Spirit-controlled man. This, of course, is the first law.

2. You will practice what you teach to your children.

3. You will be regular in your daily Bible reading. For children, Bible reading is *caught* more than *taught*.

4. You will lead family devotions. Without referring to yourself as the "priest," you bring God into your home.

5. You will protect your family against unseen enemies. Read Ephesians 6:10–18 to remind yourself of the spiritual warfare that threatens your family.

6. You will care for your wife spiritually. God has entrusted her to you. (See Ephesians 5:25–26.) No one on earth can help—or hinder—your wife in her spiritual walk as much as you can.

Husbands and fathers, your spiritual authority is paradoxical. Like the authority of the Lord Jesus, it is devoid of pride and ego, and yet confident. For the rest of your life, you will have daily opportunities to give of your energy and love—and the recompense is glorious.

SPIRITUAL POWER FOR YOUR FAMILY: PRAYER

(Prayer of a Spirit-empowered husband)

> *Father God, please establish me as the spiritual leader of my household. I want You to teach me how to love my wife as Your Son, Jesus, loves and cares for His body, the church, and lays His life down for her.*
>
> *I also want You to make me more aware of Your fatherhood in my own life so I can be a better father to my children. May I have no regrets about the years I have been a father, even when I make mistakes, because of Your forgiveness and saving power.*
>
> *I surrender myself to You, Lord.*
> *In the strong name of Jesus, amen.*

CHAPTER 9

Leading Your Children to Christ

WITH THE WHOLE scope of family life in mind, I have entitled this chapter "Leading Your Children to Christ." Leading your children to Christ involves much more than bringing them to a saving knowledge of Jesus Christ, although that, of course, is a vital step. Leading them to Christ involves every aspect of your family life and every stage of your children's development. From before your children's births until long after they have left home to make a life for themselves, your heart's desire will be for them to know and love the Lord and "to walk in truth."

"Family" is God's idea. "God sets the solitary in families" (Ps. 68:6). Like everything else He has created, families do not exist merely for their own benefit. God's purpose for every family is that its members, especially the children, receive the care they need to become full-fledged citizens in His kingdom.

However, because human beings have been raising families since Adam and Eve, we may be influenced by the idea that it's "natural" to know how to do it. I don't think so! In fact, anyone who has already started a family knows how difficult it is to bring up children. We will fall short even with the most expert advice in the world. In raising our children for Christ, we need more than advice—we need the ever-present assistance of the Spirit of God. "Unless the LORD builds the house, they labor in vain who build it" (Ps. 127:1).

MAKE YOUR HOME A HAVEN OF LOVE

To be led to Christ, children need to know they are loved, from their earliest moments through every circumstance of their growing-up years. The home of a Christian family should be a particularly secure haven of love because of the love of God Himself. ("God is love" [1 John 4:8].)

Children not only gain a sense of self-worth from being loved by their parents, but also love insulates and protects them from the fiery darts of the evil one and his emissaries in society. With a loving "home base," they will always know the difference between darkness and light, and their consciences and instincts will be trained toward godliness.

Such love takes time—sacrificial time. It does not happen by accident or by default. You cannot adequately express love without spending time doing it. Don't believe the argument that "quality time" can be a few minutes a day. Both parents need to be present to their children many hours of most days to achieve the kind of secure love that cannot be shaken.

I strongly recommend that the after dinner/early evening time should belong to the family (not to the TV). Fathers who take time each evening when they are home to read stories to their children not only enable them to become good readers, but they also show their children that they are deeply loved. For good family bonding and to teach fairness, parents should make time to play games together with their children. And as the children mature, parents who show an ongoing interest in their schoolwork and their interests remain actively involved with their training and nurture. Your children don't care if you are the president of a bank or the dean of a college, but they will never forget that you made time for them because you loved them.

In your earnestness about wanting to follow God's plan for your family life, try to avoid thinking about your family life in terms of "shoulds" and "oughts." Family life is like any other category of life— only successful by continually living by the power of the Holy Spirit. We fall down and pick ourselves back up, with His help. We aren't following a rulebook; we are following our Lord and Savior. It is our joyful obligation to become as free as we can be in Christ Jesus and to teach our children His way of new life. Your children can come to know God as well as—or better than—you do, but only if you keep the fire of love burning brightly in the family hearth.

SO RICH IN LOVE

Your children will see God's love in action if you and your spouse love each other well. They need to see that the two most significant people in their lives love each other intentionally, daily, and through ups and downs. A husband who cherishes his wife is a living example of how God cherishes each of us. A wife who respects her husband shows her children how to respond not only to their dad but also to their heavenly Father.

Your children are your mission field, and your behavior at every hour of the day or night makes such a difference. How many times have we—for better or for worse—found ourselves duplicating the behavior of one of our own parents? Our influence over our children is incalculable.

You and your spouse may want to take some special time to talk and pray about your marriage and family life. If you don't already do it on a regular basis, together ask God to bless your household.

Wherever you find "sticking points," those nagging difficulties that seem to crop up too often, ask God to help you with them. Maybe you didn't grow up with very good examples of marriage and family life. That's all the more reason to get on your knees together before the Lord. He will help you. "A cord of three strands is not quickly broken" (Eccles. 4:12, NIV). One strand is the husband. One is the wife. And the third is God Himself, binding you together in perfect love—that is true spiritual power!

Any Christian parents, from the poorest to the richest, can give unconditional love to their children. If you happen to be very poor in material goods and feel you can give too little to your children, take hold of God's love with both hands and give it to your partner and your children. Loved by the most important person in their lives, they will all flourish and rise above any shortcomings.

When we were young in the ministry, trying to get a good start in a small church, I remember going to visit one of our parishioners who was ill. We wound around little dirt roads looking for an address but couldn't find it. There were no road signs and no house numbers. Finally, we came up to a small wooden cabin-like structure, and when we knocked on the weather-beaten door, a familiar face opened it and greeted us with a warm smile. We entered into a one-room house that served as a bedroom, living room, and kitchen, with a potbellied stove right in the middle of the floor. They invited us to come in and sit down, offering the only chairs they had, orange crates turned on their sides. The family consisted of the mother and father and their three children. But they didn't feel poor. They had the most remarkable love for each other and for the Lord. The conversation that day was centered on how good God was and how He had helped them through many trials. We have visited in many wealthy homes with the best of earthly possessions, but never have we sensed the depth of family love as we did that day sitting on orange crates. They were so rich in love!

Incredible but true, nothing can ever separate us from His love.

"Neither death nor life, nor angels nor principalities nor powers, nor things present nor things to come, nor height nor depth, nor any other created thing, shall be able to separate us from the love of God which is in Christ Jesus our Lord" (Rom. 8:38–39). *Nothing* can separate us from His love, even the faulty expressions of love within our homes.

Don't listen to the insinuations that the enemy would like to plant in your mind: "You are an awful parent." "You can't possibly love your spouse or child right because your parents didn't raise you right." You can love, because He loves you. Pick up the Book of Romans, which reminds you, "The love of God has been poured out in our hearts by the Holy Spirit who was given to us" (Rom. 5:5).

ON THE OFFENSIVE

With this goal of making your home a haven of love, how do you handle the inevitable conflicts and challenges inherent in family life? Every husband and wife represent a different set of characteristics, sins, and weaknesses. Their children do, too. We need to be aware of patterns and problems so we can tackle them with God's help before they become unmanageable. Most of them represent aspects of basic human nature.

Courtesy

For example, since children are not automatically courteous, we will need to train them in basic social behaviors. They will not learn common courtesy unless their parents teach them. Too many children are growing into adulthood today without the faintest idea of how to be polite and good-mannered. They want everyone to listen to them when they talk, but they have no concern about interrupting when others are speaking. Their thoughts center around what best serves their interests. How do we change that? By constantly teaching them to be thoughtful of others, starting when they are very young and continuing until they leave your home.

Starting when children are still small, parents should insist on the use of "please," "thank you," and "excuse me." In general, children should not be allowed to interrupt adults in conversation. Their parents can defer interruptions with a simple phrase, "Please wait a minute until I'm finished speaking with this person." When parents and children make a habit of practicing courteous habits at home, it is easy to behave this way in other situations.

Even if your child is an only child, teach him or her how to share possessions. We all need to unlearn our "Me first!" inclination. I have devoted all of chapter twelve to the topic of overcoming selfishness, since it is so important to happy family life.

Fears

Children have many fears and insecurities, which vary with their age, personalities, and experiences. Adults do too, of course. Once they spot fears in themselves, adults can ask for God's help to overcome their own fears even as they work to assure that their children don't inherit them. "There is no fear in love; but perfect love casts out fear" (1 John 4:18).

Fears blind us to God's ever-present love and protection. Some fears are obvious, such as a child's fear of darkness or the mysterious bumps in the night. Others are much more subtle and hard to detect. The biblical equation is simple: Fear $\neq$ Love. Whenever you see fear, you can assume that God's love is lacking. Ask God to help you identify fears in your family so you can bring them into the light of the saving love of God. He will replace your fears with His peace.

Because fears are such an impediment to our personal and family lives, I discuss them more in depth in chapter eleven, "Power Over Fear."

Anger

Parents get angry at each other and at their children, and children get angry back. Believing that anger is wrong doesn't keep it away.

I discuss anger in much more detail in the next chapter, "God's

Remedy for Anger." For now, I simply wanted to mention it as an intruder into the home of a Spirit-empowered family. In your home, whatever does not manifest the fruit of the Spirit (Gal. 5:22–23) is an unwelcome visitor, and the Spirit will help you escort it out the appropriate door.

TEMPERAMENTAL JOURNEY

The recipe for every family includes the spicy mixture of the individual temperaments of the family members. Whether our children are our own flesh and blood or are adopted, we have to work at getting to know what makes them tick. Regardless of how many children you have, each one will have a different temperament from his or her brothers and sisters. The genes that aid in determining the blend of temperaments come from two parents, four grandparents, and eight great-grandparents.

Failing to understand our differences can give rise to untold grief in family relationships, because we are guaranteed to be different from each other—even opposites. You can comprehend much more than you would think about the temperaments of your children and how they interact with yours and that of your spouse.

In a general way, what can you learn about your own children from reviewing the four principal types of temperaments? Remember that the first two types are more introverted and the last two are more extroverted.

If your child is primarily *melancholic*, he or she can be very gifted, with a sensitive, artistic nature and a bright mind. The downside of this is that his or her feelings may be easily hurt. As a parent, you will need to be extra-encouraging with this child. His or her potential to be an outstanding adult makes your loving efforts worthwhile. As the word *melancholic* suggests, this child may be prone to depression. Over the years, depression and its host of related feelings can lead to addictive behavior, as the child attempts to find relief. Your melancholic child will probably be a perfectionist, and you will need to offer frequent reassurance of your unconditional love. Parents may find that, depending upon their own temperaments, they may disagree about how to discipline their melancholic child. Almost always, one parent feels the other is being too lenient.

If your child is primarily *phlegmatic*, he or she may be relatively easy to bring up. Quiet, calm, and easygoing, this is the child who doesn't need a lot of attention, even as an infant. When a conflict occurs, this child will most likely find a way to sidestep it rather than enter the fray. This child will often play with food at a meal instead of eating as fast as the rest of the family, and he or she may want to have an exclusive right to playthings. One spark in this tame picture may be teasing; phlegmatic children can become masters of the art. Easily influenced by their peers, phlegmatic teens need parental nudges to go in the right direction. By and large, phlegmatic children become pleasant adults, although it is very important that they learn responsibility during their growing-up years so they can successfully handle the freedom of adulthood.

If your child is primarily *choleric*, he or she will be unusually self-sufficient from an early age. Unlike the phlegmatic sibling, who quietly digs in his heels when he wants to disobey, the choleric child will loudly and angrily proclaim his disapproval. This is the proverbial "strong-willed child." Parents should assert their authority with confidence and consistency, aiming not to throttle the spirit of this child (whose leadership traits can serve well in adulthood) but to bring the will of the child into concerted obedience. This child will be an energetic organizer of neighborhood activities. However, with increased maturity, it will become more difficult for this child, whose motto is "I can do it myself," to depend upon the Holy Spirit. The choleric child is the most difficult to lead to faith in Jesus after the age of about twelve. Before that age, however, this child is quite responsive.

If your child is primarily *sanguine*, you will know it right away by the stream of chatter. This is the child who rides in the grocery store cart asking strangers, "Hi, what's your name?" This is also the child who most often hears "Shhhhh" from his parents and teachers. The world is the sanguine child's stage, and he or she will find many ways to become the center of attention. They may get carried away with their stories and merge them with exaggeration or untruths. Often daredevils with a short attention span, sanguine children keep their caretakers on their toes. You will be pleasantly surprised to find that your sanguine child is eager to please you. Don't be dismayed, however, at how easily he or she forgets an earlier resolve, promise, or punishment.

❧ ❧ ❧ ❧ ❧

There is no one else on the face of the earth (past, present, or future) exactly like your child, even if he or she is an identical twin. So don't force your children into some preconceived notion of what they should be like. Let them be unique. They won't be just like you or your spouse, and they certainly won't be like the "average" child in the child-rearing books. You will be a more relaxed parent if you can enjoy the gift of uniqueness.

Personal Salvation Experience

God has so planned it that every person shall give an account of himself to his heavenly Father. Therefore, it is essential for children to have their own conversion experiences. If we, as parents, could invite Christ into our children's hearts by the effort of our own faith, doubtless we would. But each child must experience and respond to God's invitation personally when he or she can understand with knowledge, believe with the heart, and assent with the will. As we have all heard, "God has no grandchildren," only first-generation children who have believed on their own.

For children who are raised in a Christian home, that experience may occur at a very early age. That was the case with our daughter Linda, who was very responsive to spiritual things. She understood basic biblical truth sufficiently to invite Jesus into her heart at four years of age. After she grew up and had her own children, all three of them received the Savior at nearly the same young age. Others of our children waited until they were six or seven years old.

Parents should be sensitive to the spiritual yearnings of each child. Do not pressure them, lest their desire to please you (or rebel against you) influence the integrity of their decision. On the other hand, older children should be an increasing object of prayerful concern by their parents if they have not received Christ before their twelfth birthday.

Various studies have shown that more than 80 percent of believers make their decision for Christ during their teenage years or before. Most of these decisions were made because of the influence of one or both Christian parents, who witnessed to their faith unobtrusively and naturally in the context of day-to-day life, exercising it as they confronted challenges and teaching it through Bible stories and church involvement.

Wise parents will occasionally give opportunity for their young children to rehearse their conversion experiences in order to keep them fresh and personal in their minds. The Bible counsels us, "Let the redeemed of the LORD say so" (Ps. 107:2). Children need to hear how their parents came to Christ as well and to be told about the events surrounding the conversion of their brothers and sisters.

Individual conversion is the most basic spiritual experience for a Christian. If parents take this step for granted, their children may enter the precarious stage of puberty without it.

FROM DIAPERS TO DIPLOMAS

The process of raising a child to adulthood is so complex that people are always churning out advice. It is far beyond the scope of one book to cover it all. Let's do a quick survey of the process of raising a child to adulthood, touching on important points that relate to the power of the Holy Spirit.

Babies and toddlers

God has given parents a special place in the hearts of their children during their early years when they can teach them almost anything. Each child goes through the most important stages of development during the first few years of his or her young life. You are programming your child for future attainments in all categories of his life: intellectual, spiritual, and relational. This period moves forward with great speed.

Your child's learning begins at the moment of birth. Very quickly, your child acquires his basic outlook on life and develops either a basic sense of trust and security or one of fear and insecurity. Again let me say that it is so important for the mother and father to be the caretakers of the child during his preschool years. You will never regret that special time spent during your child's most critical stages of development. As your baby develops, you need to be protective but not overprotective. Find interesting playthings, and watch what your little one will do with them. Even plastic tubs and car keys make good toys. Your role is to provide an environment of safety and consistency, where needs are met in a wise and timely way. Even with seemingly mundane matters, you can ask the Holy Spirit to show you what to do.

Loving discipline. For a child to get his or her own way regularly is worse than a steady diet of candy. But human nature insists on it, and almost every child tries. That is why your loving discipline is so important. If your child doesn't learn at home to control his impulses and desires, he will grow up to be a self-guided missile headed for disaster.

The effectiveness of discipline, including judicious spanking, is confirmed by all good parents and by the Bible itself. (See in particular the Book of Proverbs, noting Prov. 13:24; 22:6; 23:13–14; 29:15.) Modern child-rearing techniques make much of a child's so-called intuitive grasp of right and wrong, fairness and unfairness. Too much burden is laid upon the poor parent to determine what degree of fairness is appropriate. Heaven forbid that you should give an unfair command; you fear that your child's rebellion may be justified if you do it incorrectly. The Bible, however, does not say, "Children, obey your parents when they are right." It says, "Obey your parents in the Lord, for this is right" (Eph. 6:1). Surely parents will seek to be fair, but all of us are ever so fallible.

To what end do we discipline our children? To the end that our old, carnal natures become subject to the power of God within us. We learn how to come to the cross again and again to lay down our sinfulness and receive forgiveness and fresh life.

Consistent example. Children are the world's greatest imitators. They act out of what they see at home. Angry, selfish children emerge from angry, selfish homes, and loving, joyful children come from Spirit-directed homes. Integrity, honesty, industriousness, and consideration for others are both taught and "caught" by children as they grow up. A parent's consistent example is so powerful that its influence can extend even to the third and fourth generation. (See Exodus 20:5.)

Consistently immerse your children in the Word of God. Scripture memorization can begin as early as you start reading and singing to your children. Simple, one-line verses are the best. "The joy of the Lord is your strength" (Neh. 8:10). "Do all things without complaining" (Phil. 2:14).

Teach them to practice replacing the wrong response with the right one. For example, if they become upset when you tell them to do something, furnish the right response for them: "Here's what you should say—'Yes, Mom, I'm coming.'"

School age

The school-age years comprise most of a child's growing-up years. Academic accomplishments accrue at a rapid rate, and children's personal differences begin to become pronounced. Experts say that 80 percent of your child's capacity for learning will have been developed by the time he or she is eight years old.

Because children are so responsive to intellectual stimulation, don't let them vegetate in front of the television or computer games. Provide them with as many educational outlets as you can, and ask for God's guidance as you decide about their schooling. Public school, private school, or homeschooling may all be viable options for you, or some combination over the years. Your child's temperament as well as your own gifts and temperament will help you decide what is best.

Work vs. play. When children are still young, they love to do "grownup work." It's an honor to be asked to help Mommy or Daddy with a chore. Later, however, the appeal of work changes. Once I watched several boys work very hard to clear an ice rink of snow before they played hockey. If their fathers had asked them to expend the same amount of energy shoveling the driveway, they would have begrudged the time and effort of so much "work." With good humor, parents can press home the lesson that work is good and that a good attitude about it is even better.

It is important for your children to learn that there is no "free lunch." Someone has to pay for everything. By showering their children with too much wealth, well-meaning parents often teach them that anything they want can be obtained without effort. Children need the responsibilities of chores around the house in order to get an allowance and the joy of earning extra money to buy something they want.

We have a friend who has worked for decades with inner-city youth. In addition to helping them spiritually, he has tried to help them find work. He told us he has to get the kids started working early, when they have a natural instinct to do so. He said, "If you wait until they are nineteen before they get their first job, even if they have been genuinely converted to Christ, it is almost impossible for them to keep their jobs."

Work is a four-letter word for children when it comes to keeping their rooms clean and tidy. There are always exceptions, of course, but as a rule the parents need to decide how much friction their relationship can handle over this matter. Sometimes circumstances will be on the parents' side. One parent related to me a story about her daughter, whose room was a disorganized mess. One evening when the family was away, their burglar alarm sounded, and the police came. Moments later, their college-age son came home and found the police walking around the outside of the house. One officer said, "I think I found the room where they entered; it looks like it's been ransacked." You guessed it—it was his sister's room in its normal chaotic disarray.

Spiritual growth. Spiritual sensitivity is keen during the school years. Without forcing a decision upon your children, be ready to answer questions about heaven, God, death, and sin. Any of these years may provide the right moment for their clear decision to follow Jesus. Ask God to keep you sensitive to His Spirit and to your children, in case you should need to invite them personally to ask Jesus into their hearts. Your prayers and faithful teaching, including attendance at Sunday school, will lead your children to an early acceptance of Jesus Christ as their Savior.

One of the best things you can do for your child is to find a good church. The church is the one place a family can go where the values they are trying to instill in their children at home will be supported and reinforced. All parents need that outside voice—the pastor, Sunday school teachers, youth leaders—to reaffirm the biblical standards their children hear about at home.

Physical growth. Needless to say, these years are also a time of rapid physical growth. For a parent, besides keeping up with feeding and clothing their children, this means answering questions about sexuality. If you and your spouse model a healthy relationship with each other, this will go a long way toward instilling healthy standards into your children. As the middle-school years approach, boy-girl interest will increase greatly. If your child isn't asking you questions, he or she is probably getting his information from his friends or the media. Ask a few leading questions of your own. It's far better that your child should have straight facts from you than the distorted version of the truth.

More than facts, of course, your child needs a clear moral grounding. Children will not get this in most public settings. By the time they are twelve years of age, they should know that the pleasures of intercourse should be reserved for marriage because they can have serious consequences otherwise.

The school years can be fun years. Your children are old enough to interact with you in discussions, work, and play. This time will be what you make it. I have to chuckle when I hear my now-grown kids tell others that we have always had some family tradition or other. Sometimes I can't even remember doing the thing, and often I didn't realize they had become "traditions" because they were created spontaneously out of the loving fellowship of our family during the school years.

Teens

Children eagerly anticipate their thirteenth birthday; parents often dread it. This day signals entrance into the adult world. This period of time requires more parental involvement than ever.

You should build on what you have started. No other time of life is stormier than this one, and as teens shift between immaturity to maturity (sometimes many times a day), they need the solid grounding of wise parents with whom they can relate. If you did your parental homework when your children were small, raising teenagers can be fun. But if you wasted the opportunities to bond with them, mold their character, and enrich their temperaments, you will have your work cut out for you for the next five or six years. As James Dobson has wisely stated, "The time to disarm that teenage time bomb is before he is five years old."

Peers. Pray for your teen's friends, and get to know them yourself. Don't make the mistake of letting your son or daughter select friends who remain invisible to you. Peer pressure influences teenagers for good or for bad, and it is probably the greatest pressure our children will ever face. "Evil company corrupts good habits" (1 Cor. 15:33).

Pray that your teens will attract and be attracted to godly friends and good role models. Pray for their non-Christian friends to become believers. The biblical injunction to not be "unequally yoked" (2 Cor. 6:14–15) is meant to apply to marriage, but it can apply also to a teen's closest friends. These friends should be believers, because "the righteous should choose his friends carefully, for the way of the wicked leads them astray" (Prov. 12:26).

This applies even more to "more than just friends," or dating. Turn to chapter eleven for more on this hot topic.

Morality. The teenage years are characterized by experimentation with immorality. Temptations lie around every corner, whether or not your teen attends public school. Obviously, the world at large and the public school system do not teach moral principles; they will have to be taught and modeled at home, supported by the church. The challenges are enormous.

Again, the only way to succeed is to start early. Have you helped your child develop a sensitive conscience in matters of morality such as lying? Have you encouraged your youngster from the time of his or her conversion to develop an ongoing pattern of repenting for wrong thoughts and actions? Does your child enjoy a basic trust relationship with you as parents? Does your child have healthy interests and activities and a sense of responsibility about working? If so, the attraction to teenage temptations such as drugs, sex, or alcohol will be much weaker.

One of the strongest antidotes to immoral behavior is an invigorating spiritual life. Some of the most successful teens I have ever known were surrounded by other "on-fire" kids who were downright excited to be following the King (and I don't mean Elvis).

The moral values of your community are set by its leaders, not its people. For too long, Christians and other morally minded citizens have sat on the sidelines, ignoring local and state elections, not recognizing that those people decide what is legal in their communities. I believe every parent has a responsibility to his children, his God, and his neighborhood to be a voting citizen. Do your part to make sure that your public leaders share your family values.

Insecurity. One of the reasons that peer pressure is such a problem for teens is that they are not yet secure in themselves. They need more encouragement and understanding from you than ever, even though they may make themselves obnoxious at times. Avoid becoming a professional critic. A mother of several teenage boys once said, "I have one modest goal: to say one positive thing to each boy, each day." At the time, her friends' children were all younger, and this comment seemed to them to be particularly uninspired. However, as time went on and they all had teenagers of their own, they appreciated the advice. For parents of teens, the temptation to nag and criticize is very strong indeed.

Keep in mind that your teens' need for your approval is increasing, not decreasing, even as they become more independent of your day-to-day care. Give your approval honestly and often. Approval from both mother and father is the most important factor in the development of security and maturity.

From the elementary school years on through high school, give your children opportunities to try new things, and try some of them yourself. None of you may ever become an expert, but you can say you tried them. If your teen happens to excel at some sport or music or even whitewater rafting, the feeling of accomplishment in that area will provide a big boost to overall confidence.

❦   ❦   ❦   ❦   ❦

Your family is your most important possession. You must carefully protect it as if your life depends on it, for the lives of your children do. It is still possible to raise a family to love and serve God today, but it takes more effort and time than it ever has. Make your family your highest priority, and with God's help, you and your loved ones can make it.

Many people say, "If I had my life to live over, I would spend more time with my family." You will never hear anyone say, "If I had my life to live over, I would spend *less* time with my family."

Make time today to do something with a family member.

Spiritual Power for Your Family: Prayer

Lord,

Unless You give us wisdom, persistence, and love, we will never be able to bring our children up to love You. You know all of the impediments better than we do. As we try to be good parents, please help us again and again. May we never forget to turn to You with every need. Help us to discern good from evil and to be sensitive to the quiet voice of Your Holy Spirit.

We ask You to train us in righteousness as well as wisdom. Even as our children grow, may we continually grow in maturity and responsiveness to You.

Our lives, and the lives of our children, depend on Your care.

In Jesus' name and because of His saving love we pray, amen.

Part Three

Spirit-Empowered
Solutions
to Family Problems

CHAPTER 10

God's Remedy for Anger

ANGER (WITH ITS cousins, fear and selfishness, which we will consider in the next two chapters) represents one of the biggest enemies of successful marriage and family life. Until it is identified and overcome by the help of the Holy Spirit, anger can infect, damage, and even destroy the loving relationships between husband and wife, parents and children, and siblings. It takes many forms, not all of which are obvious or volatile.

Even when anger is strong and well entrenched, Spirit-empowered families can triumph over it. By learning to identify what anger looks like in their particular situation and by surrendering it to God, Christians can enter into the fullness of life that God intends.

You cannot conquer anger by ignoring it. It will not go away. It may change to a new disguise or it may go underground for a while, but it will not disappear—until you personally and intentionally bring it to the cross of Jesus Christ.

You can't dethrone anger by excusing it, either. ("It's just my Italian blood.") We must recognize that very little of the anger in our marriages and families is so-called "righteous anger." Most of it, like a skin disease that's characterized by red flare-ups, is caused by the underlying infection of *sin*, common to mankind. (See Romans 3:23; 1 Corinthians 10:13; Hebrews 12:1.) A Spirit-filled man or woman needs the help of God to look at his or her anger resolutely and to see it transformed into the fruit of the Spirit.

MASTER OF DISGUISE

Anger is a master of disguise. What you recognize as anger in your spouse may not be your type of anger at all. Some people may even think they have no problem with anger, although by the time most people have been married awhile—and especially after they have children—they may be shocked to see how much anger resided in them all along.

To better unmask anger in your own life, skim this partial list of "disguises":

- Addictions
- Agitation
- Animosity, enmity
- Annoyance
- Argumentativeness, contentiousness
- Bitterness, jealousy
- Competitiveness (excessive)
- Criminal behavior (vandalism, theft, or worse)
- Criticalness
- Deceitfulness
- Defensiveness
- Discontent
- Displeasure
- Exasperation

- Fretfulness
- Fury
- Gossip, slander, backbiting
- Grumpiness
- Hard feelings
- Hostility
- Impatience
- Indignation
- Intimidation
- Irritation
- Legalism
- Malice (wishing harm on another)
- Manipulativeness
- Passivity, refusal to accept responsibility
- Peevishness
- Petulance
- Rage
- Resentment, offense
- Resistance, rebellion, stubbornness
- Revenge
- Rudeness (intentional)
- Sarcasm
- Sulking
- Withdrawal, withholding affection (including running away)
- Wrath

That's quite an unpleasant list, isn't it? Anger, in any of these forms and others, corrupts the fruit of the Spirit in us (Gal. 5:22–23). It steals our joy. It cripples our ability to live a Spirit-directed, abundant life together in our marriages and families.

TEMPER AND TEMPERAMENT

The ways we express anger will be colored by our individual temperaments.

In brief—*melancholic anger* is slow burning and may involve vengefulness. *Sanguine anger* flashes hot but is easily forgotten after an outburst. *Choleric anger* is turbulent and may reignite over the same issue later. *Phlegmatic anger* represents a contradiction in terms, since people with this temperament rarely become perturbed unless their temperament mix includes one of the other three types. When a phlegmatic person gets angry, look for a quieter expression, such as stubborn resistance.

Our basic temperament differences aren't the whole story, however. From a young age, people make choices that influence their degree of anger and their ways of expressing it. Scripture says, "In your anger do not sin" (Eph. 4:26, NIV). Most of us don't resist sin very effectively. We don't know any better. We follow the path of least resistance, and we become very skilled at justifying our behavior.

Friends and family members learn how to sidestep each other's anger, often reacting with some anger of their own. In any neighborhood, we can find at least one mother who specializes in exploiting her adult children, putting big *guilt trips* on any who fail to cater to her demands. Her children end up becoming bitterly resentful at such treatment. Meantime, a group of her friends seek "anger relief" by gossiping behind the backs of the people they disagree with. Down the block lives a family that tends to keep the windows closed so no one will hear their squabbles. As the father in that home explodes like a firecracker, his wife and children learn to stand a safe distance away. In a nearby home, the father never raises his voice at all, but his wife and children have learned to resist his nitpicky personal criticisms. And of course there is the old guy (there's one in every neighborhood) who is as characteristically grumpy as a three-year-old who hasn't had a nap.

With so much anger marching around inside and around us, what can we do? Most of us know that suppressing anger merely creates another mutation of its expression. We certainly cannot run away from it for very long. Are we trapped in an endless cycle of hurtful outbursts and tense peace, with our relationship problems compounded by our anger-related health ills?

"It's Eating Me Up"

Obviously, anger isn't good for us. Yes, in a primitive sense it may help us see threats and motivate us to the necessary *fight or flight*, but even then, it's taking a toll on our bodies and minds. Doctors would be out of business if it weren't for the effects of the stress of protracted anger. Our bodies and minds are resilient, but only up to a point.

It is staggering to recognize how many days a year Christians lie in hospital beds and how many millions of dollars are wasted by God's people on unnecessary illnesses, not to mention how many people have been turned away from faith in Christ by believers whose anger repels rather than attracts others. This includes, of course, the children of Christian parents. Who knows better than a family member what *really* goes on in each family when they're not sitting in the pew on Sunday morning? Our homes are meant to be an emotional haven of love, peace, and joy to which couples and their eventual children can resort, shielded from the hostile, selfish world outside. Unfortunately, many people find more hostility and animosity in their homes than outside them.

Sometimes, we don't realize that anger is at the root of a problem. I'm thinking of a wife who complained to her pastor, "I have lost all loving feelings for my husband." After her pastor probed a bit, he discovered that they had recently had a major disagreement—over the purchase of a garbage disposal, of all things. Her husband had refused to buy her one, saying that his mother had never had one, and he didn't see why any woman should need one. She had become infuriated and resentful. In no time—*poof!*—her feelings of love for him had vanished.

All she had to do was repent of her angry reaction. It didn't matter whether or not it was "justified." Her angry reaction was choking off her marriage. She confessed and repented and went home to love her husband again. The footnote to this true story is that within several weeks, without any further discussion of the matter, he surprised her with a brand-new garbage disposal.

MARRIED AND ANGRY

Most couples return from their honeymoon basking in the sweetness of their love. They continue that way awhile—until they experience their first conflict or clash of wills, a "lovers' quarrel." Usually, the first one isn't fatal, although it leaves a slight scar on their bliss. And making up is such fun!

So they romp down the marital pathway for another stretch of time—until another clash, and another. These conflicts can start to come closer and closer together, especially after the birth of children, until their loving home becomes a hell on earth.

No one has to tell a married couple that men and women are different. They know from firsthand experience. But they often don't know how to resolve the inevitable disagreements that make their marriage into a battleground.

We hear the truism, "Opposites attract." Often a husband and wife represent not only opposite genders, but also opposite temperaments and gifts. One may be an extrovert and the other an introvert, one gifted with verbal expression and the other with deductive ability. One may be neat and the other messy, and so on.

This is a positive arrangement in one regard because we tend to admire people who are strong in areas in which we ourselves are weak. Once we are married, we hope the other person's admirable qualities will be able to compensate for our lack. Of course, our subconscious expectation is dashed when we discover the pitfalls of those strengths. Then the temptation is to look disdainfully or contemptuously upon our partner's weaknesses. Anger flares up, and then it moves in to stay, taking new forms as children come along.

160

MARRIED AND ANGRY, WITH CHILDREN

Parenting is surely one of the most difficult assignments on earth, and there has never been a perfect parent except God the Father Himself. (I'm assuming that even Mary and Joseph made some mistakes as they raised Jesus.)

Anyone who has children, whether they are still infants or are now grownups, has regrets about some aspect of the child-rearing years. So often our regrets have to do with the way we have mishandled discipline or decision making, two types of situations where anger can enter easily. Whether we have blown up like volcanoes or kept ourselves at a slow simmer, our anger has made an indelible impression on our children.

God holds us responsible to provide a loving environment for our children, one in which their inevitable sinful reactions can be tamed with His help. That's why He made sure Paul wrote the words of Ephesians 6:1–4:

> Children, obey your parents in the Lord, for this is right.
> "Honor your father and mother," which is the first com-
> mandment with a promise: "that it may be well with you
> and you may live long on the earth." And you, fathers, do
> not provoke your children to wrath, but bring them up in
> the training and admonition of the Lord.

While agreeing heartily that this is God's Word to us, we can fail miserably at following it. Is it inevitable that we will repeat the mistakes of our own parents?

Here is our new baby, fresh-faced and relatively pure—well, "pure" if you discount his natural selfishness and tendencies to rage loudly when "I/me/mine" is not serviced instantaneously.

And here are his parents, bleary-eyed, blundering, and short-tempered after being up all night with their new little one, struggling to balance the demands on their time and energies.

From the beginning, it doesn't sound like a recipe for successful parenting.

And yet, paradoxically, such struggles are God's way of leading us to step #1 of the successful recipe: "Recognize that you cannot do it by yourself." Our sinful muddling and failures can be the best thing that ever happened to us—if we recognize that not only do we need help, but also that God Himself will provide it.

When Jesus said, "I am the way, the truth, and the life. No one comes to the Father except through Me" (John 14:6), He meant that by allowing Him to live in our hearts, we ourselves can begin to embody the way, the truth, and the life. We don't do it by searching desperately for answers in the Bible, self-help books, or elsewhere. We do it by walking with Him as our closest companion.

Walking in constant interchange with His Spirit, we will find our way out of the anger traps as well as all the others that litter the path. It may take some time, especially if we didn't know about the Holy Spirit early in life and we have more course correction to achieve, but it can happen.

A good part of course correction within the family context will involve discipline. When I have discussed the subject of discipline with other parents, I have found that many times, "discipline" is little more than angry lashing out. Parents, angered by some perceived misstep on the part of the child, spontaneously strike their child or yell. Even though they may recognize that this is wrong, they don't know how to change. They don't look beneath their anger for the hurt or disappointment that may have fueled such a reaction. They certainly don't take steps to remedy the damage (because they are still too angry).

When our two sons were young, one of them had disobeyed, and Tim, in his frustration and anger, mistakenly punished the wrong boy. After realizing what he had done, he took the wronged boy in his arms and said, "I'm sorry, Son, I made a mistake. Will you please forgive me?" The boy said, "Of course, Dad; I know you're not perfect." What a sad but tender moment that was between Dad and his son, and also a lesson that when we make mistakes, we can go to the Father and ask for forgiveness. I have often thought that if my husband had not asked our son to forgive his mistake, a root of bitterness could have grown out of that action of anger. Instead it was a blessed time of father and son bonding closer together.

Parents who desire to practice effective discipline in their homes will first have to get victory over their own anger and hot tempers. (At the end of this chapter, I have provided some practical steps that help.) Then, picking themselves back up each time they fall, they will continue to walk with the Lord and continue to let Him transform them into His character likeness.

Without undercutting the child's respect for the parent's status, a Spirit-filled parent can repent of inappropriate anger to children (of any age), and all of them can climb back onto the path of love. Such humility goes a long way to establish the parent as a godly example for the child. The child, seeing a clear example, can repent if necessary and forgive the parent for real or perceived unfairness. Often quicker learners than their parents, children can outstrip their parents' low expectations for this process. Children who learn how to handle their anger will not resort to passive-aggressive expressions of it, and they even may be able to help their siblings and others learn how to take unruly emotions to Jesus.

A wise parent will learn what it means to not "provoke your children to wrath" (Eph. 6:4). Sometimes, it is a matter of strategy, circumventing anger-producing situations wisely and without surrendering parental authority or consistency. For example, everyone knows that two-year-olds are notorious for asserting *NO!* to every request. A wise parent can eliminate some of the potential tension by changing a yes/no request into a special opportunity for the child to exercise his or her budding independence. If you want your two-year-old daughter to drink a glass of milk with her lunch, don't say, "Honey, here's your milk. Please drink it." (Response: *NO!*)

Instead, appeal to her equally strong desire to make her own decisions: "Sweetheart, would you like your milk in a blue glass or a yellow one?" She chooses a color and drinks her milk happily—one less argument for the day.

At any age, the most difficult thing is *wanting* to conquer anger. Our emotions are strong, and they interact with others' emotions all too quickly. Once again, we need God's help—and He hastens to give it when we ask.

> How gracious he will be when you cry for help! As soon as he hears, he will answer you. Although the Lord gives you the bread of adversity and the water of affliction, your teachers will be hidden no more; with your own eyes you will see them. Whether you turn to the right or to the left, your ears will hear a voice behind you, saying, "This is the way; walk in it."
>
> —ISAIAH 30:19–21, NIV

WHAT TO DO ABOUT ANGER

God does not leave us clueless as to how to deal with our anger. The Bible is His instruction book. In it, we see stories of angry people (for example, Cain, Moses, King Saul, the apostle Peter, Saul of Tarsus) from which we can learn, either by positive or negative example. We also find an abundance of practical advice, some diagnostic ("A quick-tempered man does foolish things, and a crafty man is hated" [Prov. 14:17, NIV]) and some prescriptive ("Do not let the sun go down while you are still angry, and do not give the devil a foothold" [Eph. 4:26–27, NIV]). It is the latter kind of advice that helps us know what to do about our own anger and how to help our children with theirs.

The first step is always the same: no one can gain true victory over anger without first being reborn into the kingdom of God. Every born-again believer becomes a new creation in Christ Jesus (2 Cor. 5:17). As a result, every time his or her old nature reasserts itself, a Christian can tap into the supernatural power of the Holy Spirit. As people who have been transferred out of the kingdom of darkness into the kingdom of light (Col. 1:13), we can walk free of sin. In fact, Scripture says we are "dead to" it (Rom. 6:11), and it is no longer our master (v. 14).

Several practical steps will help born-again believers become increasingly free of anger. Every time you become angry (or you see its fruits of turmoil, which should make you suspect hidden anger), take yourself through these tried-and-true steps:

1. *Face your anger as sin (Eph. 4:30–32).* You cannot overcome it if you don't face it. Confronting your behavior as sin is the first giant step toward a cure. If you justify or excuse your anger, you are not confronting it as sin.

2. *Confess your anger as sin (1 John 1:9).* You need to verbalize the fact that your anger is wrong and you wish to be rid of it. God's ear is always attuned to the cry of the sinner, the psalmist tells us, and He is quick to forgive.

3. *Confess that God is bigger than your anger, and that He can help you (Rom. 5:20; 1 John 2:1–2).* This is called a "positive confession." It will build your own faith that God is fully able to save you from your sin, even when you feel discouraged and beaten down by it.

4. *Ask for forgiveness for your sin (Ps. 32:5).* When anger rises, acknowledge it as wrong, confess it to Jesus, and ask to be forgiven for it. If you have harmed anyone (including verbal harm), you may need to ask for that person's forgiveness as well. This includes asking your children to forgive you if you discipline them in anger.

5. *Ask God to take away this habit pattern (1 John 5:14–15).* Anger is not only a sin, but it also becomes a habit. You have spiritual power from God to overcome old habits as well as old sins. Anything you ask Him to do that is within His will, He promises to do. It is His will for you to be free

from the sin of anger. The habit may reassert itself, but each time you ask God for help, it will become weaker.

6. *Ask for a new filling of the Holy Spirit (Luke 11:13).* As some teachers say, tongue-in-cheek, "We may be filled with the Spirit, but we leak." Ask God to replenish your spirit with His Holy Spirit. Tell Him you want to be new, through and through.

7. *Give thanks for the source of your irritation (1 Thess. 5:18).* Thank God in and for the circumstance that caused you to become angry (Eph. 5:19–20), realizing that it happened for your good (Rom. 8:28). It may not have been good in itself, but God turns it for good every time. Gratitude is a good way to deflect your mind from dwelling on what happened, so you won't fall into anger once again.

8. *Repeat this series of steps every time you get angry.* Habits won't disappear overnight. But as you apply yourself to these steps, they will gradually melt away. After awhile, you will become a new person—and you will enjoy the results of God's transformation!

It sounds almost too good to be true, but it is true, nonetheless. Anyone, even an enraged Saul of Tarsus, can be transformed into a saint.

SPIRITUAL POWER FOR YOUR FAMILY: PRAYER

O Lord,

I do cry out to You for help, and I know You hear me. Whether I am overwhelmed with the anger in my own life or merely troubled by a recent incident, I know You want to renew me with Your Spirit's love and set my feet on the right path.

As I journey along, please lead me to the "wells" of Your Word that will sustain me. Show me how to offer refreshing "drinks" to my family members. Motivate me to get back up on my feet when I fall and to make it possible for my spouse and children to get back up also.

I am grateful for all that You have taught me, even the hard lessons. I acknowledge Your lordship over my life.

I pray in the name of Jesus, amen.

CHAPTER 11

Power Over Fear

FEAR HAS BEEN around a long time. It is the first negative emotion mentioned in the Bible. After the Fall, Adam told God, "I was afraid...so I hid" (Gen. 3:10, NIV). Before sin entered the picture, Adam and Eve had not known what fear was. They felt secure and content. But ever since their sin infected the human race, fear has acted as a destroyer.

Fear is not confined to an isolated experience. Rather, it becomes a way of life. Fearfulness makes people worry about almost anything that is new and different, and sometimes also about familiar things. Fearfulness inhibits people relationally, vocationally, socially, educationally, sexually, and spiritually. It corrupts prayers into sanctified worrying or consecrated complaining.

Fear is evoked by the unpredictability of the real and imagined dangers of life. We experience fear when confronted by something dangerous or new. Every one of us is subject to some kind of fear—even those of us who are afraid to admit that we are afraid!

For some, it gets out of hand. Doubtless, you know someone who has refused to learn to drive a car in spite of having had ample opportunity. They have good excuses. What is the *real* reason they do not want to try that new thing? Fear. They realize that driving doesn't require special intelligence or superior reflexes or mechanical ability. However, it does take a degree of courage that they lack. A fear-prone person will not allow himself or herself to attempt activities that arouse that uncomfortable feeling of fear.

We all know people who are afraid to get married or to have children. We may know people who are afraid to apply for a job, any job. Every local church recognizes that a large number of its membership have never taught Sunday school or vacation Bible school, or participated in any of its outreaches or programs. It's not just because people are too busy—it's mostly because of apprehension and insecurity (two synonyms for that stark word *fear*). The same people can't take advantage of witnessing opportunities—because they are afraid. Most of them would love to share their faith and lead others to Christ, but fear seals their lips.

Fear stifles conversation and communication in the home. It hampers many parents from insisting on standards and guidelines, and it occasions many family squabbles, especially as children become more independent. Many parents make the fatal mistake of being afraid to discipline their teenage children. In spite of believing the biblical principle that "evil company corrupts good habits" (1 Cor. 15:33), they are afraid to say, No! Stop! or Quit! What are they afraid of? Perhaps that their teen won't love them or will leave home?

Fatigue exacerbates fears. All adults have experienced the unreasonable fears that run through one's mind at 3:00 a.m., while the rest of the family sleeps. While most adults aren't too concerned anymore about large monsters under their beds, their hearts still beat harder when they hear an ominous bump in the night.

Some people are characterized by so much overt fear that they are known as "worrywarts." It can become even more extreme than that. Even if we have not experienced them ourselves, we have all read about "panic attacks." And then there are phobias, paralyzing fears about specific objects or places such as a fear of snakes or of heights or of tight spaces. *Fear* is everywhere.

EQUAL-OPPORTUNITY ANXIETY

We don't realize how ubiquitous fear is because different kinds of people are plagued by different fears. Our temperaments have a lot to do with the different fears we experience. Phlegmatic people can become anxious worriers. A person who is melancholy may be most afraid of criticism, insults, injury, and even fear itself. Sanguine folks are less afraid; they may even be daredevils. But they tend to be insecure, so their fears center around pleasing other people. People with a choleric temperament have the fewest fears, but since most people aren't 100 percent choleric and everyone suffers at least a few fear-producing life circumstances, most of them have some fears to conquer.

Each person's temperamental predisposition is influenced by the environment in which that person grows up. In an ideal family situation, the parents will be able to recognize their own besetting fears well enough to obtain God's overcoming help for them. They will be able to help their children grow up in a secure home where love, consistent discipline, and wise instruction help their children grow to maturity of character. The same basic temperament can go either way. The child's personal and spiritual growth will be stunted if the parents supply rejection, lack of discipline, or unreasonable dominance.

Whether we realize it or not, we have choices about how we react to our environments and experiences. Inevitably, most of us choose to react to fear-producing situations out of our human resources rather than in the power of the Holy Spirit, especially when we are still young. As a result, we develop fear-based habits. We start to believe that our reactions are "just the way I'm wired." We don't realize that God provides a way out.

ANGER AND FEAR IN MARRIAGE

So often, Anger marries Fear on a couple's wedding day. When the calm, easygoing types are drawn to hotheaded, quick-tempered spouses, and when warm, personable kinds of people are attracted to cool perfectionists, the fear inhibitions of one temperament cause disagreements with the other.

In addition, the fears of childhood, which may have been hidden during courtship by the romantic excitement of being in love, may emerge after marriage. As the routine of daily living becomes established, collisions are inevitable. Regrettably, sometimes the fear-anger dynamic can become so intolerable that the couple may divorce on grounds of "incompatibility." Such incompatibility is nothing more than fears and anger driving in a repeated collision course.

Couples can generally adjust to each other's temperaments and predispositions, but even if they have adjusted, they should consider how to conquer the fears that remain in them as individuals. If their relationship is good, each one can provide a safe place for the other to emerge from hiding and into God's restoration.

DO NOT BE AFRAID

Although we live in a world characterized by uncertainty and have been *programmed* to react in fearful ways, worry and anxiety do not have to accompany us to our deathbeds. God wants us to become free of them and to learn to trust Him reflexively, as a small child trusts his daddy. He wants us to have confidence and inner peace and to find new joy that can be our enduring strength.

What do you think is the most frequently stated commandment in the whole Bible? "Don't sin"? "Believe in God"? "Love one another"? Believe it or not, the most common instruction in the Word of God is, "Do not be afraid." God addresses human fear more than 365 times, enough for us to read a new statement every day of the year. He doesn't address our fear because He is irked with us about it. Far from it. He wants us to be reassured that He is in charge and that we can lay down our fears at His feet. Consider this sampling of passages from both the Old and New Testaments:

> Have I not commanded you? Be strong and of good cour-age; do not be afraid, nor be dismayed, for the LORD your God is with you wherever you go.
>
> —JOSHUA 1:9

> When you lie down, you will not be afraid; yes, you will lie down and your sleep will be sweet. Do not be afraid of sud-den terror, nor of trouble from the wicked when it comes; for the LORD will be your confidence, and will keep your foot from being caught.
>
> —PROVERBS 3:24–26

> Peace I leave with you, My peace I give to you; not as the world gives do I give to you. Let not your heart be troubled, neither let it be afraid.
>
> —JOHN 14:27

CHECKING THE FOUNDATION

Before I move on to some steps to cure fear, I want to make sure that everyone who is reading this belongs to God wholeheartedly. Without a true conversion experience, we have no foundation upon which to build our freedom. I know how people skip ahead in a book sometimes, looking for a chapter that speaks strongly to them. The title of this chapter, "Power Over Fear," may have caused some of you to do just that.

Here is how to make sure that you belong to God and have become a dwelling-place for His Holy Spirit:

1. Receive salvation by repenting of your sins and inviting the Lord Jesus into your life (Rom. 10:13). The only way you can have your sins forgiven is by doing this.

2. Ask for the infilling of God's Holy Spirit (Eph. 5:18).

3. Become sensitive to His voice (Eph. 4:30–32). He will let you know when you have sinned, and He will also encourage you.

4. Repent each time you sin (1 John 1:9). When you sin, you put yourself on the throne of your life. When you repent, you allow the Lord Jesus to resume His seat on that throne; you let Him be in charge of your life.

5. Read the Word regularly (Heb. 4:12–13). You need to spend at least fifteen minutes a day reading the Bible in order to grow in your walk in the Holy Spirit.

THE CURE FOR FEAR

A good many of the fear-related biblical references remind us about God's desire to set us free from it. For example:

> If you live according to the sinful nature, you will die; but if by the Spirit you put to death the misdeeds of the body, you will live, because those who are led by the Spirit of God are sons of God. For you did not receive a spirit that makes you a slave again to fear, but you received the Spirit of sonship.
>
> —ROMANS 8:13–15, NIV

> God is love, and he who abides in love abides in God, and God in him.... There is no fear in love; but perfect love casts out fear, because fear involves torment. But he who fears has not been made perfect in love.
>
> —1 JOHN 4:16, 18

> Blessed is the Lord God of Israel, for He has visited and
> redeemed His people, and has raised up a horn of salvation
> for us...to grant us that we, being delivered from the hand
> of our enemies, might serve Him without fear.
> —LUKE 1:68–69, 74

The cure for fear is almost identical to the cure for anger (chapter ten). Here are the steps to true freedom:

1. *Face your fear, worry, and anxiety as sin.* Romans 14:23 says, "Whatever is not from faith is sin." You cannot overcome fear if you don't face it. Confronting your behavior as sin is the first giant step toward cure. If you justify or excuse your fear, you are not confronting it as sin.

2. *Confess your worry, fear, and anxiety as sin (1 John 1:9).* You need to verbalize the fact that your fear counters the liberty of the kingdom of God and that you wish to be rid of it. The psalmist tells us that God's ear is always attuned to the cry of the sinner, and He is quick to forgive.

3. *Confess that God is bigger than your fear and that He can help you (Rom. 5:20; 1 John 2:1–2).* This is called a "positive confession." It will build your own faith that God is fully able to save you from your fears, even when you feel discouraged and beaten down by them.

4. *Ask for forgiveness for your sin (Ps. 32:5).* When you act out of fear, acknowledge it as wrong, confess it to Jesus, and ask to be forgiven for it. If fear has caused you to make unwise decisions, you may also need to ask for the forgiveness of others who have been affected by your decisions or actions.

5. *Ask God to take away this habit pattern (1 John 5:14–15).* Fear is not only a sin; it becomes a habit of mind. You have spiritual power from God to overcome old habits as well as old sins. Anything you ask Him to do that is within His will,

He promises to do. It is His will for you to be free from the sin of fear. The habit may reassert itself, but each time you ask God for help, it will become weaker.

6. *Ask for a new filling of the Holy Spirit (Luke 11:13).* Ask God to replenish your spirit with His Holy Spirit. Tell Him you want to be new, through and through.

7. *Give thanks to God that every situation you face is under His control (1 Thess. 5:18).* Gratitude is a good way to deflect your mind from dwelling on what happened so you won't fall into fear as easily again.

8. *Repeat this series of steps every time you become fearful.* Habits won't disappear overnight. But as you apply yourself to these steps, they will gradually melt away. After awhile, you will become a new person—and you will enjoy the results of God's transformation!

My Story

One of the reasons I have devoted an entire chapter to fear is because I know from personal experience how it damages the fabric of family life—and how it feels to be free.

Like many young couples, Tim and I "stoked each other's fires." After we were both filled with the Holy Spirit, we began to change. His habitual anger began to be replaced by God's love, peace, and self-control. My habitual fears and insecurities began to be replaced by God's secure love, sure peace, and "sound mind" (one of the terms used in 2 Timothy 1:7, often translated as "self-control": "For God hath not given us the spirit of fear; but of power, and of love, and of a sound mind" [KJV]). This, of course, did wonders for our marriage. It also transformed my ministry outside our home.

Prior to this, my work in the church had been exclusively with children in the sixth grade and younger. Although I felt confident and capable doing this, I never wanted to address adults. As time went on, however, I gradually began accepting speaking engagements at women's events and then for larger audiences of all sorts. Eventually, motivated by the needs I saw around me, I founded Concerned Women for America in 1979, which became the largest pro-family organization in the United States. This propelled me into new endeavors, including testifying on behalf of Supreme Court appointees, appearing many times on television (sometimes with unfriendly audiences), and hosting my own radio program.

The power to overcome my natural timidity and insecurity came entirely from the Holy Spirit, who continues to give me faith instead of fear. My part is to cooperate with Him.

This may seem like a small matter to someone who is relatively fearless, but another personal example of God's power combined with intentional faith involved water activities. My family had taken up the sport of waterskiing—but not me. I had never learned to swim, and I was afraid of the water. My husband had written about my deliverance from the fear of public speaking in a book that became required reading for the trainees of a missionary board. One day, the director of the mission board wrote to Tim, thanking him for the book but identifying a significant inconsistency: "You tell how God delivered your wife from her fear of public speaking, but later you admit she couldn't join you and the rest of the family in waterskiing because she was so afraid of the water. The problem is that our nonswimming missionary candidates readily identify with her and use her as an excuse for not learning to swim, which could prove fatal to some of them as they float down the Amazon River. Isn't the fear of water just as much of a sin as the fear of anything else?"

Tim let me read the letter. After a few days, I got on the phone and arranged some swimming lessons. I purposely chose a heated swimming pool and an instructor who I knew would be patient and kind to me. I even started out by wearing a rubber wetsuit and a lifebelt, and I went to my lessons quoting to myself, "I will never leave you or forsake you." Although I will never qualify for the Olympics, eventually I did develop a less fearful attitude toward water. Since then, I have gone on many family vacations that involve water and was able to enjoy them. God can conquer our fears.

Practical Help for Fears

Many fine books have been written by Christians about how to conquer fears. Since I am devoting only one chapter to the topic, I want to concentrate on one particular set of fears that sooner or later will come home to roost in your family. Like the examples above, this is written from personal experience, and, best of all, it really helps to negotiate the uncertain ground of teenagers and the opposite sex, surely terrifying territory for many parents.

Fears About Older Children and Dating

Parents' greatest fears are often associated with the teenage years, especially with dating and sex and the risk of drugs. As early as junior high, peer pressure for dating is a strong influence, particularly on girls.

Somehow, this stage of family life almost always catches both parents and children unprepared. The teens have no idea what their parents expect of them, and the parents are not always in agreement with each other. Whereas we prepare our children for almost every other arena of their lives with schooling, lessons, or at least helpful tips, we seem to tiptoe around the whole issue of relating to the opposite sex.

Dating causes fear in many parents' hearts for several reasons. First, it represents a giant step toward independence. Parents lose a large degree of control over their teenager when he or she goes out for hours at a time. Second, many parents have not learned to trust their children, and dating accentuates that lack of trust. Third, they have not prepared guidelines in advance, so the independence of dating exaggerates their fears. Fourth, with the increasing experimental use of drugs for teens, it is absolutely necessary for the parents to prepare their young people ahead of time as to what their reaction should be.

We have found that if the first child in a family is coached and prepared before launching into this stage of life, it is a relatively simple matter to get younger brothers and sisters to accept the same standards. But if parents strike out with number one child, they may also lose with the others.

Having developed and tested guidelines for dating on ten children, four of our own plus six missionary children whose parents sent them to live with us for their junior and senior years of high school, I'd like to suggest them for other parents.

Guidelines for dating

1. *No dating under the age of sixteen. Dating* means a boy comes to a girl's home to take her on a specified outing. Most states don't give out driver's licenses before that age, anyway. Many families require their sixteen-year-old drivers to pay for their own car insurance (which can be a staggering figure) before they can take the car. Reserving dating until the age of sixteen is no problem for boys, because they may be busy working trying to earn enough to pay for insurance, and many boys are not interested in girls until much later. Girls are another matter. Because they mature faster than boys, both physically and socially, they are often anxious to start dating very early. Unfortunately, with so many boys their own age disinterested or without drivers' licenses or money, girls look to older boys—which presents a new set of problems.

2. *Date only Christians.* Dating can be a prelude to marriage. The Word of God clearly spells out that believers should not be "unequally yoked together with unbelievers" (2 Cor. 6:14). The way to help your young son or daughter avoid the emotional trauma of either marrying an unsaved person or

having to break up is to set a standard at the very beginning, before any emotions get involved. This standard may cause a few tears when your daughter is forbidden to keep company with the handsome high school quarterback with whom she is infatuated, but it will eliminate a major trauma later.

3. *Schedule a predating interview with the father.* This really sorts out the kind of guys that want to date your daughter! Any young man who dates your daughter is *borrowing* one of your most treasured possessions. If he borrowed your car or boat, you would clearly set some guidelines for its use. How much more important is this with your own daughter? This step may scare some prospects away, but you will not regret it. Any boy who lacks the courage to look a girl's father in the eye when asking permission has no business dating her anyway. This interview gives the father the opportunity:

   a. ...to see for himself that the young man is really a Christian. (Hearsay testimonies aren't always valid.)

   b. ...to check his vision for his own future. Do you detect a sense of responsibility and self-discipline in him? Is dating your daughter and getting her alone his only objective for the moment?

   c. ...to clearly lay down the guidelines they are to follow. Don't expect your daughter to do this. It is embarrassing for her. Besides, something can easily be missing in the transmission of information.

   d. ...to size up the home life from which the lad comes. The answer to this question may not necessarily determine whether they can or cannot date, but whether or not the young man loves and respects his parents helps you to know what to expect in your relationship with him.

When your son wants to date a Christian girl, it is somewhat easier for you to share with him your guidelines, which are essentially the same as those for girls. He then sets the standards with the girl he goes out with. If he dates the same girl two or three times and you haven't yet met her personally, you would be wise to have him bring her along to meet you and your spouse. (I suggest that the mother may be in on this interview because often a woman can better evaluate another woman.)

4. *All dates must be approved in advance.* Until young people get acquainted with you and your guidelines, don't let them stampede you into a quick approval of some type of activity of which you do not approve. We made it clear to our teens that approved dating could include all church activities and outings, chaperoned parties, sports events, and special events they wished to request. The "don't even bother to ask" list included movies, dances, unchaperoned private parties, or any activity where drinking or drugs were involved. (We included movies and dances in this list for several obvious reasons. Most movies have some sexual overtones, even the PG-13 movies, and dancing is often combined with alcohol or drugs. Our prohibition eliminated the chances of our children finding themselves in a compromising situation.)

5. *Until high school graduation, double-date only.* This is one standard the kids objected to the most. But we felt there was some safety in numbers. The main reason for this, however, is to force them to make plans in advance and to keep them from being alone for long periods of time when they could drift into "heavy couple talk." Under the romance of the moment, it is easy to make premature love statements and engage in physical touching that can lead to sexual intercourse. The presence of another couple cuts down on this possibility drastically, although it doesn't eliminate it entirely. Because it is admittedly difficult to get up a double

date, we compensated for our stringent rules by bending over backward to make the family car available. Usually the one with wheels can find someone to double-date with him.

6. *Absolutely no "parking"!* Every locale has an area where young people gather and park their cars. Some may be very pretty places, but they are not good environments for resisting youthful temptations. We believe dating is for fun and social fellowship, not for purposely tempting teenage self-control. You may ask, "Didn't your children ever park during their dating years?" We aren't so naïve as to think they didn't, but if they did, we wanted it clearly understood that it was against our rules.

7. *No public show of affection.* Love is beautiful, but public demonstrations of affection that border on suggestiveness cheapen the reputation of the couple. The Christian community applauds teenagers who obviously love each other but who have enough self-respect not to maul each other in public. Besides avoiding "all appearance of evil" (1 Thess. 5:22, KJV), open expressions of affection today may prove embarrassing later when romantic interest in that person has faded.

8. *Curfew.* Ours was 11:00 p.m. for our girls and 11:30 p.m. for our boys (to allow them time to escort their dates home). We made exceptions for certain functions that we knew in advance would last later than that. Our early curfews were universally resisted at first because they were earlier than those set by most parents. But our reasoning was that there is very little wholesome activity going on in our city after 11:00 p.m.

The problem for parents may be how to enforce the curfew, which will likely be ignored, and how to handle the ensuing conflict. We solved it by saying that every minute they were late would cost them 15 minutes off their curfew for their next date. One young man brought our daughter home so late that their next date was only a little over an hour long.

These guidelines may seem too rigid to you, but even modified guidelines may help to reduce your fears as a parent (and your child's fears as well). Communication is the key. The teenage years are full of emotional instability. Fears thrive where communication is absent or angry. Whatever you do, keep the lines of communication open with your older children.

LIVING A FEAR-FREE LIFE

God gives us a blueprint for fear-free living in the Book of Proverbs. A good part of His instruction involves hungering for and employing true wisdom, developing sound judgment, and relying on simple common sense. It seems likely that He would not have devoted so many words to overcoming fear if most people don't really need the help.

In addition, we need reminders, lots of them. Achieving a fear-free existence takes time and effort, and if our circumstances crumble around us, we may need to relearn the same lessons again.

Superficial teaching has conditioned us to think that the goal of the Christian life is abundant material provision plus circumstantial "smooth sailing." Somehow, this never quite works. Even if we happen to achieve a trouble-free existence for a brief period of time, soon the fallen world we live in will encroach on our bliss. If nothing else, illness, aging, and death will serve as reminders that we need God every hour.

Each and every one of us needs to keep leaning into His love, "for God has not given us a spirit of fear, but of power and of love and of a sound mind" (2 Tim. 1:7).

SPIRITUAL POWER FOR YOUR FAMILY: PRAYER

Lord God,

I want Your Word, especially the truth You have spoken about our fears, to go deep into my innermost being. To help accomplish that, I will read and repeat the scriptures that You draw my attention to.

Help me also to act on Your Word, by the power of Your Holy Spirit, so that I can leave my fears, worries, and anxieties behind and walk into fresh, trusting life with You.

I pray for _____ [name family members], *whose fears only You can conquer. I trust that You will use my prayer for his/her greatest blessing and use me to be a loving influence on his/her life.*

With great gratitude and forward-looking faith, amen.

CHAPTER 12

Overcoming Selfishness

I N ADDITION TO anger and fear, the third basic marriage and family problem is selfishness. We are all born with it, and to one degree or another it plagues us throughout life. God's Holy Spirit wants to help us become increasingly unselfish as we become better rooted in His love.

Every baby is born with a self-centered attitude: "I am the only child on earth, and you must cater to my needs!" This is normal because babies are immature. However, unless selfishness is trained out of the little person through his parents' patient love and discipline, he or she will remain immature into adulthood. Selfish people are not only less suitable as marriage partners, but they will also have trouble finding contentment in their circumstances and in their relationships. An egocentric person thinks of himself first and foremost in everything.

As with anger and fear, selfishness is expressed in different ways by different types of people. No temperament type is exempt from tendencies toward selfishness. A sanguine man or woman has an ego that is hungry for attention at all times. Choleric people selfishly run roughshod over others or use them for their own purposes, casting them off afterward. They are also prone to anger, which is another expression of selfishness. People with melancholic temperaments tend to be self-centered, evaluating everything from the standpoint of "what's good for *me?*" Phlegmatics, pleasant as they can be, are nevertheless overprotective of themselves, often afraid of being hurt or offended, and they are apt to be stingy.

Although it may find expression in different ways, selfishness permeates all types of people through and through, and it distorts all aspects of personal and family life.

HOW TO LIVE UNHAPPILY EVER AFTER

Happiness depends upon learning to share one's self, time, talents, and possessions with others. *Happy* is another word for *blessed* throughout the Bible. Remember Jesus' words recorded by Matthew:

> Then the King will say to those on His right hand, "Come, you blessed of My Father, inherit the kingdom prepared for you from the foundation of the world: for I was hungry and you gave Me food; I was thirsty and you gave Me drink; I was a stranger and you took Me in; I was naked and you clothed Me; I was sick and you visited Me; I was in prison and you came to Me."
>
> —MATTHEW 25:34–36

Human beings can achieve a degree of unselfishness on their own, but to become truly unselfish requires being "un-selfed" by means of a new birth experience and a filling of the Holy Spirit. When we find a new home in Christ Jesus, and He comes in to dwell with us, we can abandon our self-centeredness and let Him

186

launch us on the journey toward freedom from the tyranny of self.

I say "launch" because the transformation is not instantaneous. In fact, the territory of self can be conquered only inches at a time. The change is a slow process.

What are some of the domains of selfishness? A big one is always money and whatever money can buy. Selfishness also lays claim to our time usage, alters our decisions, spoils our relationships, obstructs our child rearing, influences our giving and receiving, corrupts our lovemaking, gives license to our hobbies and sports, overextends our celebration of holidays, and so on.

How to Live With a Selfish Mate

Many marriages are obvious casualties of selfishness. Even if romance overcomes selfishness to some degree during the courtship days and through the honeymoon, selfish habits weaken their love as a couple settles into married life. Divorce because of "incompatibility" is really divorce because of selfishness. Needless to say, this is far from the biblical pattern, which holds that the only acceptable reason for divorce is adultery. Although adultery can be blamed on selfishness as a root, that is as far as the reasoning goes. Any and all other selfishness-produced strife is not a valid excuse for divorce.

But even when a man and woman adopt strategies to learn to live with each other's selfishness, selfishness itself remains firmly entrenched. The hardest person to love "until death us do part" is not the one who is unattractive or who has an uninteresting personality—it's the partner who is stuck in selfishness. We can see the problem clearly where money is concerned. Money troubles come up so frequently that many marriage counselors call it the chief matrimonial issue. Self-interest and self-protection (two aspects of selfishness) defeat reasonable dialogue about finances.

So what can the Christian mate do if a selfish partner is unwilling to face his or her problem and seek God's help in overcoming it? The answer is not to go see your lawyer; it is to ask the Holy Spirit to flood you with His love, joy, peace, and wisdom. You will find that He will give you sufficient grace to live with your selfish companion. Since He promised to supply all your needs, you can depend on Him to supply grace to love, honor, and cherish that person as you promised to do on your wedding day.

Trust the Lord with your situation. Continue to walk in the Spirit, bringing your own sinful patterns to death on the cross, and let God take care of your partner. Whether your spouse decides to seek to change or not isn't your decision. Your decision should be to trust God, take Him at His Word, and walk in the Spirit daily. Each time you get angry at your spouse's selfishness, confess your anger and commit him or her to God. (If, however, your spouse's selfishness leads to adultery or abuse, do seek outside help.)

You may need to consider at least one loving confrontation about the matter. As the Scriptures say in Ephesians 4:15, you should "[speak] the truth in love." Still walking in the Spirit, you can graciously confront your spouse's sin of selfishness. One reason for doing so is to let your partner know that you do not approve of his or her behavior. A surprising number of people assume their mates realize the depth of the problem, but selfish people are usually quite blind to it. Another reason you should confront a selfish mate is because if you don't, the pressure will build up in you until you explode in anger. Then you will say too much too harshly and end up doing more damage than good.

Having once confronted the person "in love" (often difficult to do), you can commit your partner to God and expect Him to work. Even if your spouse never changes, you will become happier and freer as you continue to walk in the Spirit.

How to Bring Up Unselfish Children

Can parents successfully bring up unselfish children? Not if they remain stuck in selfish patterns of their own. But if a couple is walking together in the Spirit, their children are their primary responsibility, and God will provide abundant grace for bringing them up in the ways of the Lord.

God does not demand perfect parents, which is good news to most of us, since we fall short in many areas. But He does expect us to make every effort to bring our children into obedience. Willing obedience is the opposite of willful selfishness.

Teaching obedience requires much more than giving instructions. After the instructions, we need to insist on the child's compliance. Too many parents fail to follow through in discipline of their children. Yes, it's taxing to be so consistent. No, you can't take a vacation from it. But don't worry. It will only take the next twenty years or so of your life. (Just think how much less selfish you yourself will have become by the end of your child-rearing years!)

Your effort is worth it, even if your children, who possess free wills of their own, choose to rebel against their upbringing. In any case, starting with helpless newborns, you will have taught your children to take responsibility for their own lives, and you will have introduced them to their heavenly Father, who can carry them through adulthood.

What should you do if you are just realizing that you have been negligent in disciplining your children to help them achieve obedience? Because nothing is impossible with God, you can still move forward and make changes in your approach. Regardless of the ages of your children, consider the following words of advice, and trust that God can work on your behalf.

1. *Recognize and admit your areas of failure.* Ask God to show you where you have been weak. Be willing to name the weaknesses: pride, irritability, permissiveness, inconsistency, wrong priorities, lack of spiritual leadership, being a poor role model, and so forth.

2. *Confess your failures before God, and ask for His forgiveness.* "If we confess our sins, He is faithful and just to forgive us our sins and to cleanse us from all unrighteousness" (1 John 1:9).

3. *Confess your failures to the family members involved.* Pray that they will be able to forgive you. "Above all things have fervent love for one another, for 'love will cover a multitude of sins'" (1 Pet. 4:8).

4. *Ask God to help you change.* The Bible gives us help for changing our habits and developing new tactics to correct the problems.

5. *Trust God to work.* You can step out from under the guilt of the past, for it has been forgiven. You can expect His help as you correct your own bad habits and learn to correct the patterns that have developed in your children.

Bear in mind the heartening words of Hebrews 12:2, 5–6 (NIV):

> Let us fix our eyes on Jesus, the author and perfecter of our faith . . . [and remember] that word of encouragement that addresses you as sons:

> "My son, do not make light of the Lord's discipline,
>   and do not lose heart when he rebukes you,
> because the Lord disciplines those he loves,
>   and he punishes everyone he accepts as a son."

THE PROBLEM OF SELF-REJECTION

One aspect of selfishness that can too easily escape notice is self-rejection. Self-rejection, or "low self-esteem," may be so deeply internalized that it goes unrecognized. It adopts many faces, which vary with the individual and the occasion. Perhaps your self-rejection has caused you to strive for academic honors or athletic awards. Or, perhaps more likely, it has caused you to retreat socially and vocationally and has curtailed the free expression of your personality. In some cases, it is manifested through self-deprecation (not to be confused with true humility), or even depression. Self-rejection puts the emphasis on self.

Most of us dislike and reject at least some aspect of our appearance, our talents, our environment, our past experiences, or our future prospects. If we feel this way, doubtless we will think it's normal, since many others around us express similar sentiments. If we happen to know people who are happy to be just as they are, we have no idea how to attain that happiness for ourselves. We may even reassure ourselves that we are more "in touch with reality."

Any self-rejecting individual must come to realize that this approach to self defies God. After all, where do we put the blame for our looks, body size, temperament, or talent? On the One who arranged our genes at conception, of course. Only by admitting ingratitude, unbelief, and even rebellion against God will such people learn to accept themselves.

It is particularly helpful for people who want to be free of self-rejection to thank God *out loud* at least one time for whatever it is that they hate about themselves. If they hate their looks, they can stand in front of a mirror and thank God for exactly how they look, naming the aspects of their appearance that they most dislike. Offering these same characteristics back to God, they can ask Him to show them how He intends to use them for His glory.

I think of Gladys Aylward, a parlormaid in London a hundred years ago, who had determined to become a missionary. She had always disliked her small stature and straight, coal-black hair. Growing up with other girls who were endowed with blonde curls, she always felt second-class. Then she arrived in China. What did she see all around her? Petite women with straight, coal-black hair! A tall, blonde missionary would have looked freakish to the people, but she blended right in. To her credit, she had recognized earlier that God doesn't make mistakes. Everything He allows to happen brings Him glory in one way or another, and it can bring us great joy to appreciate His handiwork.

God can do extraordinary things with very ordinary people. There is no reason for us to reject ourselves.

The Problem of Depression

Any Christian counselor will testify that depression is one of the most common disabilities he confronts. It is probably more common than their statistics show, because for every Christian who seeks counseling, there are others who simply carry on with their lives as they might if they had a low-grade infection in their bodies.

Depression is the combined result of anger, fear, and self-rejection. Therefore, because of the transforming work of the Holy Spirit in our lives, it follows that most Spirit-filled Christians should be able to be depression-free unless their depression has a genetic or biochemical cause. In all cases, depression can be eased with the insightful, loving, and practical help of the greatest Counselor in the world, the Holy Spirit.

Dealing with depression, of course, is a process just like every other kind of growth. It entails active participation on the part of the depressed person who, in order to be set free, must put his or her hand trustingly into the mighty hand of God.

To a large extent, depression is triggered by good, old-fashioned self-pity, another one of those "self" problems that spring from unredeemed selfishness. It usually starts with provocation of some sort. A happy, well-adjusted person will not suddenly become depressed as if he had been hit by a viral infection. Usually he will be able to remember what happened—or what he remembered from the past, perhaps an insult or an instance of personal rejection.

Whenever you find yourself falling into depression, hold your circumstances up against this pattern:

Rejection/Insult/Injury $\Rightarrow$ **self-pity** $\Rightarrow$ DEPRESSION

You can transform this equation into a better one, by changing your reaction to rejection, insults, and personal injuries. Especially if you precede thanksgiving with the steps to freedom from selfishness that you will find just below (which are very much like the biblical steps to freedom from anger and fear), your outcome will be *joy* instead of depression:

Rejection/Insult/Injury ⇒ thanksgiving by faith ⇒ JOY

When we engage in self-pity because we are going through some trials and tribulations, we can remember what someone has said: "The Lord takes us through deep waters not to drown us, but to cleanse us." And then we can give thanks and experience joy.

The truest joy is born in times of the deepest struggle. Expect the blessing of joy each time you engage your enemies of selfishness, fear, anger, or depression.

THE CURE FOR SELFISHNESS

Depression, self-rejection, and selfishness are deadly enemies of a happy marriage and family life because a person's attitude toward himself will influence his attitude toward God, toward others, and toward everything he does.

Many well-meaning Christians cling to the mistaken notion that self-acceptance or love for self is unspiritual. But our Lord assumed that we would accept ourselves when He said, "Love your neighbor as yourself." (See Matthew 19:19; Mark 12:31; Luke 10:27.) You cannot love your neighbor very well if you don't love yourself very well. God's divine order is clear: Love Him supremely, then love your spouse, then your children, and finally love yourself and other people equally. If you depreciate yourself, it will lower your ability to love everyone else.

The same basic cure for anger and fear will work for selfishness and self-rejection as well. Here are the (by now familiar) steps to take in walking free:

1. *Face selfishness or self-rejection as sin (Rom. 14:23).* Admitting that selfishness and self-rejection are sinful is a major step toward becoming free of them.

2. *Confess selfishness or self-rejection as sin (1 John 1:9).* You need to tell God (out loud) that you realize your selfishness is wrong and that you wish to be rid of it. He will hear you and forgive you.

3. *Confess that God is bigger than your problem with selfishness or self-rejection and that He can help you (Rom. 5:20; 1 John 2:1–2).* This "positive confession" will build your own faith that God is fully able to save you from your selfishness, even if you feel it is an impossible task.

4. *Ask for forgiveness for your sin (Ps. 32:5).* When you notice selfishness or self-rejection in yourself, acknowledge it as wrong, confess it to Jesus, and specifically ask to be forgiven for it. If your selfishness has caused harm to another person, you may need to ask for that person's forgiveness as well.

5. *Ask God to take away this habit pattern (1 John 5:14–15).* Selfishness and self-rejection become habitual, even a lifestyle. Now that you know you have spiritual power from God to overcome any sinful habit, you can be confident that He will answer. Anything you ask Him to do that is within His will, He promises to do. When selfishness reappears, repent and ask for help again. Every time, it will become weaker.

6. *Ask for a new filling of the Holy Spirit (Luke 11:13).* Ask God to replace your selfishness with the unselfish love of His Holy Spirit. He wants you to be filled with His Spirit at all times.

7. *Give thanks to God that every situation you face is under His control (1 Thess. 5:18).* God turns everything to good (Rom. 8:28).

8. *Repeat this series of steps every time you see selfishness or self-rejection in your life.* These habitual patterns will become weaker every time. God is making you free. You will *like* the new you!

Gradually, selfish patterns will begin to fade, and a mature generosity and true love for others will replace them. Your patience toward people will grow. Increasingly, you will enjoy others, and they will enjoy you. You will find it possible to obey the "Golden Rule" and other scriptural directives, such as the following:

> Whatever you want men to do to you, do also to them.
> —MATTHEW 7:12

> Give, and it will be given to you: good measure, pressed down, shaken together, and running over will be put into your bosom. For with the same measure that you use, it will be measured back to you.
> —LUKE 6:38

> But whoever has this world's goods, and sees his brother in need, and shuts up his heart from him, how does the love of God abide in him?
> —1 JOHN 3:17

> Let nothing be done through selfish ambition or conceit, but in lowliness of mind let each esteem others better than himself. Let each of you look out not only for his own interests, but also for the interests of others.
> —PHILIPPIANS 2:3–4

Your love priorities will change, and you will begin to be able to love God first, spouse and family second, and your neighbor as yourself. True love and giving are inseparable. It will become easier to be generous with your money, time, and possessions.

A mature, unselfish person never lacks for friends, for he is so "others-conscious" that other people like to be in his presence. In the context of the family, such a person is a delight to have around the house.

A key word is *gradually*. Don't expect an instant cure for selfishness or for any sinful habit or tendency. Habit is a cruel taskmaster, and although we Christians do not have to remain "slaves of habit" as our non-Christian friends are, we do, nevertheless, often fall prey to bad habits. Every time we notice self-centeredness, if we persistently face every selfish action as sin, and follow with confession, receiving forgiveness, and becoming refilled with the Spirit, we will see positive changes—it's guaranteed.

You may even notice that your lifestyle changes. You may begin to prefer simpler things, and you will give up self-indulgent desires. As you give more of your time to others, useless occupations will drop away. In due time, the people around you will tell you that they can see the Lord Jesus in you, that you bring Him into a room when you come in.

Remember the divine promise, "I can do all things through Christ who strengthens me" (Phil. 4:13). Through the power of the Holy Spirit, you, your spouse, and your children can have victory over your greatest emotional problems!

SPIRITUAL POWER FOR YOUR FAMILY: PRAYER

Dear heavenly Father,

I believe in Your care for me—and yet it's almost too good to be true! Thank You for providing not only salvation through Your Son, Jesus, but also power through the gift of Your Spirit so that we can follow You. Thank You for Your daily presence with me. Thank You for giving me insight and wisdom.

Please keep me mindful of Your ways. Don't let me forget that You are for me, not against me, even if the enemy starts to play on my weaknesses and bring discouragement. Please surround me with people who will encourage me to keep following Your ways and teach me more about Your ways as I read Your Word.

I want nothing more than to follow You, wholeheartedly, all the days of my life and to be a beacon of Your light for my spouse and family.

Gratefully yours, amen.

CHAPTER 13

Your Family and the Fruit of the Spirit

M Y GOAL IN this book has been to show you how, by the matchless power of God's Holy Spirit, the life of any family, including your family, can become a little slice of heaven. Up to now, a good number of the previous chapters have been concerned with knotty issues and all-too-common problems of family life. Yet I do not want to leave you with a problem-ridden approach to achieving Spirit-empowered family life, even though it is much easier to diagnose difficulties than it is to cure them.

I'd much rather leave you with a goal, a vision of what your family can really become with the help of the Holy Spirit. You will be much more likely to attain a goal if you know what it looks like, and you will recognize the signs along the way that indicate you are on the right path.

The Fruit of the Spirit on Every Family Tree

Jesus told us that we would know what someone is really like by the fruit that is borne in his or her life (Matt. 7:20). Do you find good fruit or bad fruit on your family tree? To review what we are looking for, let's take another look at the good fruit listed in Paul's letter to the Christians at Galatia. Having just listed the "works of the flesh," the evil fruit of human endeavors undertaken without the Spirit—"adultery, fornication, uncleanness, lewdness, idolatry, sorcery, hatred, contentions, jealousies, outbursts of wrath, selfish ambitions, dissensions, heresies, envy, murders, drunkenness, revelries, and the like" (Gal. 5:19–21)—Paul next turns his attention toward the goal:

> But the fruit of the Spirit is love, joy, peace, longsuffering, kindness, goodness, faithfulness, gentleness, self-control. Against such there is no law. And those who are Christ's have crucified the flesh with its passions and desires. If we live in the Spirit, let us also walk in the Spirit.
> —Galatians 5:22–25

Paul gives us a picture of our goal as individual Christians who have been "[set]...in families" (Ps. 68:6), which is to live and walk in the Holy Spirit, both displaying and being nourished by the fruit of the Spirit.

Other people will know we are His own chosen children if the fruit of the Spirit is obvious on our family trees. This fruit is far more than mere decoration; it is both the evidence of our walk with Christ and our means of continued growth.

One Spirit, One Fruit

Preachers often make the point that, in spite of the nine characteristics mentioned here, the key word is singular: *fruit*, not fruits. The fruit of the Spirit represents a unified expression of the character of

God. He is one God, but with many aspects. His Spirit manifests one fruit, but with many attributes.

The fruit of the Spirit is a special hybrid of love, joy, peace, long-suffering, kindness, goodness, faithfulness, gentleness, and self-control. We never see distinctive love-fruits alongside kindness-fruits. Love is kind, and kindness is loving. There is no self-control without goodness and no joy without longsuffering patience. It's all one fruit of the Spirit.

The nine characteristics help us identify the true, mature fruit of the Spirit. For example, if it looks like gentleness, but you can't detect kindness and love, the fruit in your hand may be a human facsimile of God's true gentleness, and you can be sure that it won't last very long. Or if the fruit is difficult to bite into, and when you do, it tastes sour, you know it's not mature yet. On the other hand, if it comes off in your hand when you pluck it and it feels, looks, smells, and tastes like something you have been looking for all your life, you have the real thing, the ripe fruit of the Spirit.

Paul goes on to say, "Against such there is no law." God certainly does not need to make a law against His own characteristics of righteousness. We need laws to protect us from actions and impulses that are antagonistic to God's ways. (See 1 Timothy 1:9.) But we don't need to be shielded from the fruit of the Spirit. There is nothing dangerous or toxic about it.

TASTE AND SEE

Once we have obtained a taste of the fruit of the Spirit, we know where we are headed. Through continuing faith in our risen Savior, we enter ever more into a new way of living as individuals, families, and churches. We communicate with Him all the time, because His Spirit assists us. Increasingly, we become "crucified with Christ," living by means of faith, no longer by the laws by which we used to live before we knew there was a Holy Spirit.

The phrase "crucified with Christ" comes from a sentence earlier in the same letter to the Galatians: "I have been crucified with Christ; it is no longer I who live, but Christ lives in me; and the life which I now live in the flesh I live by faith in the Son of God, who loved me and gave Himself for me" (Gal. 2:20). What has been crucified? Our flesh. (See Galatians 5:24.) Even though we remain in our fleshly bodies and our life on earth reminds us that we are not yet in heaven, we are getting ready to meet our Savior as we walk with Him day by day. We are dying to our old, sinful habits and coming alive to the new ways of the Spirit.

Early in the process, we realize that we will not be able to bear both kinds of fruit at the same time. So we purposely say good-bye to our old ways, determining to fill our minds and hearts with God's truth.

We also discover that truth alone isn't enough. If truth had been enough by itself, the old rule-abiding Pharisees could have entered the kingdom of God. No, we have a Savior who said that He is the way, the truth—and the *life* (John 14:6). To say good-bye to sin is only half of the battle. We must be filled with the Spirit and walk in the fullness of the Spirit in order to walk in newness of life.

As we do so individually and as family members, others around us will begin to catch glimpses of the fruit of the Spirit on our family trees. They will hear a joyful refrain, feel a loving touch, hear a kind word, and notice a patient reaction. And they will recognize these life-giving characteristics as coming from the same source.

Let's look at these nine characteristics of the fruit of the Spirit.

Love

"The fruit of the Spirit is *love*..." The love of the Spirit shows itself in both the vertical dimension (toward God) and the horizontal one (toward our fellow human beings).

Love ripens especially well in families. The close quarters of the household provide a wonderful balance of warmth and nourishment. In spite of problems, and often because of them, family members grow in their love for each other. Love makes a way, and love shows us the way. Love holds on in hard times.

Love promotes communication, especially between husband and wife. It relegates problems to their proper importance, situating them beneath the goal of pleasing God. Love removes barriers to communication, making it possible to forgive and to smile. Love accepts the other person just as he or she is, without trying to make changes.

The very word *love* reminds us of Paul's well-known words about love in 1 Corinthians 13:

> Though I speak with the tongues of men and of angels, but have not love, I have become sounding brass or a clanging cymbal....Love suffers long and is kind; love does not envy; love does not parade itself, is not puffed up; does not behave rudely, does not seek its own, is not provoked, thinks no evil; does not rejoice in iniquity, but rejoices in the truth; bears all things, believes all things, hopes all things, endures all things. Love never fails....And now abide faith, hope, love, these three; but the greatest of these is love.
>
> —1 CORINTHIANS 13:1, 4–8, 13

Love colors all the other characteristics of the fruit of the Spirit: *loving* joy, *loving* peace, *loving* longsuffering, *loving* kindness, *loving* goodness, *loving* faithfulness, *loving* gentleness, and *loving* self-control. Without love, the fruit of the Spirit would be shrunken and misshapen. With love, it becomes more perfect every day.

Joy

"The fruit of the Spirit is...*joy*..." Joy is so much more than happiness. The word is synonymous with *delight.* Its three letters almost dance with gratitude.

The joy of the Spirit is not shallow or fleeting. It has deep roots because it grows in the soil of hardship and pain, even suffering. Do you realize how many times the Bible connects joy with suffering? Here are a few examples, and surely you will be able to think of others.

I am exceedingly joyful in all our tribulation.

—2 Corinthians 7:4

Out of the most severe trial, their overflowing joy and their extreme poverty welled up in rich generosity.

—2 Corinthians 8:2, niv

My brethren, count it all joy when you fall into various trials, knowing that the testing of your faith produces patience. But let patience have its perfect work, that you may be perfect and complete, lacking nothing.

—James 1:2–4

And you became followers of us and of the Lord, having received the word in much affliction, with joy of the Holy Spirit.

—1 Thessalonians 1:6

When do testings and trials bring joy? Only after they are finished? Not always. Often the trial is still underway, but the joy of the Spirit wells up anyway. It is as if the joy is more real than the pain.

The source of joy is the Lord Himself, dwelling within the Spirit-filled believer. The psalmist tells us, "Thou wilt show me the path of life: in thy presence is fulness of joy; at thy right hand there are pleasures for evermore" (Ps. 16:11, kjv). Like a well that is never dry, He wells up inside us at the most unexpected times. Our part is only to look to Him, not thinking of joy but thinking of obedience to Him and reliance upon Him.

Although repeatedly he had been a hungry, thirsty, and tired prisoner, Paul declared confidently: "The kingdom of God is not eating and drinking, but righteousness and peace and joy in the Holy Spirit" (Rom. 14:17).

Peace

We have seen that joy coexists with pain, but Jesus promises peace to follow trouble if we are walking in the Spirit:

> I have told you these things, so that in me you may have
> peace. In this world you will have trouble. But take heart!
> I have overcome the world.
>
> —John 16:33, NIV

As we walk in the Spirit, we will still have our troubles. Jesus has not promised us a bed of roses, but He has promised to deliver us from the trouble because He has overcome the world. We may sometimes feel we are walking backward because we are surrounded with trouble on every hand, but in God's perfect timing, the peace that passes all understanding will be ours.

Longsuffering

Like the qualities of the Spirit listed before and after it, longsuffering is not mild or shallow. We need the longsuffering so we can patiently wait for the peace after troubled times. The old-fashioned word *longsuffering* provides a clue about its depth of meaning. This aspect of the fruit of the Spirit provides us with patient endurance over the *long* haul. We can exhibit a supernatural stamina, whether we are being buffeted on the mission field or tested to the limit by our teenagers.

In our own meager longsuffering we see mirrored the great longsuffering of God.

> The Lord is not slack concerning His promise, as some
> count slackness, but is longsuffering toward us, not will-
> ing that any should perish but that all should come to
> repentance.
>
> —2 Peter 3:9

> Or do you despise the riches of His goodness, forbearance,
> and longsuffering, not knowing that the goodness of God
> leads you to repentance?
>
> —Romans 2:4

It is a fact that most of our spiritual battles are not spectacular at all. Even the big ones are won on the ground, inch by hard-won inch.

The enemy of our souls wants to "nickel and dime us to death."

But the longsuffering of the Holy Spirit is too much for him, especially when you add a little love, peace, and joy.

Kindness

The quality of kindness, translated as "gentleness" in the King James Version of the Bible, blends so thoroughly with the other "flavors" in the fruit of the Spirit that it is difficult to discuss it separately. Kindness is both gentle and good. It brings peace and quiet joy. Without kindness, love is empty.

Kindness, to King David, was the same as salvation:

> Blessed be the LORD: for he hath shewed me his marvellous *kindness* in a strong city. For I said in my haste, I am cut off from before thine eyes: nevertheless thou heardest the voice of my supplications when I cried unto thee.
> —PSALM 31:20–22, KJV, EMPHASIS ADDED

Indeed, "God's kindness leads you toward repentance" (Rom. 2:4, NIV), without which there is no salvation.

The kindness of the Spirit enables parents to be patient with their immature and sometimes wayward children. If they bear the fruit of kindness, they don't carry their parental burden with grim stoicism, but with compassion. Kindly, persistently, and faithfully (very much like God), Spirit-filled parents can keep offering an open door to children who disobey them. It sometimes breaks their hearts, but even then they share in God's experience. "But to Israel he says: 'All day long I have stretched out My hands to a disobedient and contrary people'" (Rom. 10:21).

When obedience fails and tensions arise, do you snap? Ask the Holy Spirit to infuse you with more of His patient, gentle kindness. Keep walking with Him, even if you stumble. I guarantee that you will reach a day when, almost miraculously, the same level of tension around you will elicit a new, Spirit-infused reaction from your spirit.

Goodness

"The fruit of the Spirit is...*goodness*..." If you look up the word *good* in the dictionary, you will find more synonyms there than for almost any other word in the English language. *Good* means, among a host of similar terms, "wholesome," "salutary," "honorable," "competent," "bountiful," "attractive," "loyal," "suitable," "healthy," "abundant," "excellent," "true," and "virtuous."

We spell and pronounce the word *good* only a little differently from the name of God. This is no accident. Jesus' response when He was approached by a rich man with the question, "Good Teacher, what good thing shall I do that I may have eternal life?" was, "Why do you call Me good? No one is good but One, that is, God. But if you want to enter into life, keep the commandments" (Matt. 19:16–17).

People often say that there is some goodness in every person. While this may be true in a general sense, I am confident that true goodness only resides in us when the Author of goodness Himself dwells in our hearts. You cannot find true goodness outside of God.

King David knew, even before Jesus said so, that goodness resided in God alone. He knew that to obtain even a taste of it, he would need God's gift of single-hearted devotion. He realized that this goodness was powerful. It could vanquish enemies and comfort the afflicted.

> Teach me Your way, O LORD; I will walk in Your truth; unite my heart to fear Your name....For great is Your mercy toward me, and You have delivered my soul from the depths of Sheol. O God, the proud have risen against me, and a mob of violent men have sought my life....But You, O Lord, are a God full of compassion, and gracious, longsuffering and abundant in mercy and truth. Oh, turn to me, and have mercy on me! Give Your strength to Your servant....Show me a sign for good, that those who hate me may see it and be ashamed, because You, LORD, have helped me and comforted me.
>
> —PSALM 86:11–17

205

One certain source of growth in goodness is God's Word. The psalmist said, "Your word I have hidden in my heart, that I might not sin against You" (Ps. 119:11).

Faithfulness

Well-meaning people who may call themselves Christians often believe that God will overlook their foibles and indiscretions and let them enter heaven anyway. They have not understood what it means to "live by faith," which is such an important standard for a Christian that the New Testament would be much shorter if all the passages about faith were deleted. We can enter the kingdom of God only by faith; in fact, without faith it is impossible to please God. (See Hebrews 11:6.)

How can we obtain this all-important commodity, faith? As with everything else in the Christian life, it is only by the infilling of the Holy Spirit that we can find the power to be faithful disciples who live by faith. Faithfulness cannot be fabricated apart from God's Holy Spirit.

"Living by faith" is not an empty platitude. It's an all-consuming way of life. To be full of faith means you are actively trusting in a God whom you cannot see but whom you nevertheless consult on a regular basis. And you do what He tells you to do, whether He shows you by His written Word or through another person or by speaking directly to your conscience. Faith is your operating system.

Faith is also your identity badge. In any context, "He's a faithful man" is a high compliment. God holds dearest to Himself those who have been counted faithful. In Hebrews 11, we read a long list of God's faithful favorites: Abel, Enoch, Noah, Abraham, Sarah, Isaac, Jacob, Joseph, Moses, Rahab, Gideon, Barak, Samson, Jephthah, David, Samuel, as well as prophets and ordinary folks who are known only to God.

Spirit-empowered parents train their children in faithfulness by teaching them to look to their Savior daily for instruction and correction. They reinforce an obedient attitude toward God through their loving discipline. Because He is faithful to accomplish every word He has spoken (Heb. 10:23), God provides both parent and child with the fruit of faithfulness. The rewards are great:

> A faithful man [or woman or child] will abound with blessings.
> —PROVERBS 28:20

> Be faithful until death, and I will give you the crown of life.
> —REVELATION 2:10

Gentleness

Sometimes translated "meekness" or "humility," *gentleness*, like all the other qualities of the fruit of the Spirit, is not a namby-pamby thing. Gentleness presupposes great moral strength and lively faith. True gentlemen and gentlewomen are not superficial or spineless, but rather they are spiritual giants who can face down every foe in the name of God's righteousness.

They know the power of the *quiet* spoken word: "A gentle answer turns away wrath, but a harsh word stirs up anger" (Prov. 15:1, NIV). They are supremely tolerant of weakness—"Be completely humble and gentle; be patient, bearing with one another in love" (Eph. 4:2, NIV); "We were gentle among you, just as a nursing mother cherishes her own children" (1 Thess. 2:7)—while being very certain about the evil of sinfulness: "A gentle tongue breaks a bone" (Prov. 25:15, NKJV).

Gentle people function on a different plane of peace in the midst of chaos. Their calm peace reminds people of Jesus, who said, "Take my yoke upon you and learn from Me, for I am gentle and lowly in heart, and you will find rest for your souls" (Matt. 11:29).

You don't take a true gentleman lightly. Moses was the meekest man on the face of the earth (Num. 12:3). Yet he repeatedly confronted mighty Pharaoh with an impossible request ("Let my people go!"), he boldly held out his staff as God parted the Red Sea that swallowed up the Egyptian army, and he led the Israelites for forty years of difficult wandering in the desert. Perhaps the best demonstration of Moses' strength-in-meekness came after he disobeyed God at Meribah and God forbade him to enter the Promised Land after all (Num. 20:1–13). With true meekness born of long association with God's Spirit, Moses accepted this heartbreaking verdict.

May we all display, to the greatest degree possible, the same humble gentleness that comes from long association with the Holy Spirit.

Self-control

Self-control may seem like an odd quality to list along with all these sweeter and grander characteristics. And yet this kind of self-control is different. This is self-control under the *Spirit's* control. The self-control of the Spirit enables us to control all of those sinful tendencies that Paul listed just before he listed the qualities of the fruit of the Spirit. Without self-control, those sins can erupt without warning, especially in the context of marriage and family life. Self-control reins them back in and shows them who is in charge.

Peace, gentleness, kindness, and goodness are in jeopardy without the vigilant monitoring of self-control. Anger, fear, and selfishness, the three enemies of the Christian family that we have considered in depth in previous chapters, run rampant wherever self-control is missing.

> Like a city whose walls are broken down is a man who lacks self-control.
>
> —PROVERBS 25:28, NIV

With self-control at the helm, your ship can move ahead at full speed, even in the time of storm.

ABUNDANT FRUIT

Do you see what an unmerited gift God has given us? He has given each of us a full portion of His Holy Spirit, by whose inexhaustible strength we now walk into fullness of life, bringing our families along with us.

May the fruit of the Holy Spirit be so well displayed in our personal and our family lives that the world around us will know that Jesus is the saving Lord for all who call on His name. Peter summed up what we should do:

> For this very reason, make every effort to add to your faith goodness; and to goodness, knowledge; and to knowledge, self-control; and to self-control, perseverance; and to per-severance, godliness; and to godliness, brotherly kindness; and to brotherly kindness, love.
>
> —2 PETER 1:5–7, NIV

As I have been asserting throughout this book, Christian families can reach heights of happiness by faithfully obeying the Holy Spirit as He shows them, daily, the little "obediences" that make up a life of faith.

Whenever something disturbs the calm of your spirit, ask Him what to do. Ask Him to speak to you clearly. Surrender yourself once again. The more you apply yourself to this, the faster you will grow spiritually. Even if your marriage and family life are in such turmoil that you don't know where to begin, *He* knows where to begin. He delights to answer specific, humble prayers such as "Lord, show me where to begin obeying You, for the sake of Your name and for the sake of my family."

Expect to see signs of growth, including:

1. Gratitude in the face of any circumstance

2. A sweetness of spirit that makes people want to be around you and that carries you through hardship

3. Calmness instead of worry, anxiety, anger, or fear, even in times of crisis or confusion

4. An ability to ignore offenses and a willingness to let others have their way

In other words, look for the opposite of the three big enemies of family happiness—anger, fear, and selfishness.

Walk in the Spirit, hand in hand with your spouse and children. Don't strive and struggle to "get it right," but rest in your relationship with the Lord. As I said before, the fruit of the Spirit is both the means of growth and the evidence of growth. If you see some fruit, expect to see more. It will increase. This is quite different from a human self-improvement venture.

The people around you and your family will know you belong to Jesus Christ when they see your love, joy, peace, longsuffering, kindness, goodness, faithfulness, gentleness, and God-centered self-control.

Spiritual Power for Your Family: Prayer

As you pursue the goal of the upward call of God, which Paul talks about in Philippians 3:14, this is my prayer for you and you family:

> *Now may the God of peace Himself sanctify you completely; and may your whole spirit, soul, and body be preserved blameless at the coming of our Lord Jesus Christ (1 Thess. 5:23).*
>
> *Because of Jesus and through the power of His Spirit, amen.*

For more information about
Concerned Women for America
such as…

- General information about the organization.
- How to become a member and receive the monthly *Family Voice* magazine.
- How to get in touch with a local CWA chapter or prayer-action group.
- Where to hear current CWA webcasts & news updates.

Write to:
Concerned Women for America
1015 Fifteenth Street, N.W., Suite 1100
Washington, DC 20005

Call:
(202) 488-7000
(800) 458-8797

Web site:
www.cwfa.org

Additional Books by Beverly LaHaye

The New Spirit-Controlled Woman (Harvest House)
Strength of a Godly Woman with Janice Crouse (Harvest House)

Books With Tim LaHaye
The Act of Marriage (Zondervan)
The Act of Marriage Over 40 (Zondervan)
Raising Sexually Pure Kids (Multnomah)

Fiction Series With Terri Blackstock (Zondervan)
Seasons Under Heaven (vol. 1)
Showers in Season (vol. 2)
Times and Seasons (vol. 3)
Season of Blessing (vol. 4)

Strang Communications, the publisher of both Charisma House and *Charisma* magazine, wants to give you 3 FREE ISSUES of our award-winning magazine.

Since its inception in 1975, *Charisma* magazine has helped thousands of Christians stay connected with what God is doing worldwide.

Within its pages you will discover in-depth reports and the latest news from a Christian perspective, biblical health tips, global events in the body of Christ, personality profiles, and so much more. Join the family of *Charisma* readers who enjoy feeding their spirit each month with miracle-filled testimonies and inspiring articles that bring clarity, provoke prayer, and demand answers.

To claim your **3 free issues** of *Charisma,* send your name and address to: Charisma 3 Free Issue Offer, 600 Rinehart Road, Lake Mary, FL 32746. Or you may call 1-800-829-3346 and ask for Offer # 93FREE. This offer is only valid in the USA.

---

www.charismamag.com